# FORBIDDEN KNOWLEDGE TRAVEL

Published by Adams Media, a division of F+W Media, Inc.
57 Littlefield Street
Avon, MA 02322
www.adamsmedia.com

ISBN 10: 1-4405-0199-8
ISBN 13: 978-1-4405-0199-9

Printed in China

This publication is designed to provide accurate and authoritative information
with regard to the subject matter covered. It is sold with the understanding
that the publisher is not engaged in rendering legal, accounting, or other
professional advice. If legal advice or other expert assistance is required,
the services of a competent professional person should be sought.
—From a Declaration of Principles jointly adopted by a Committee of the
American Bar Association and a Committee of Publishers and Associations

Many of the designations used by manufacturers and sellers to distinguish
their product are claimed as trademarks. Where those designations appear in
this book and Adams Media was aware of a trademark claim, the designations
have been printed with initial capital letters.

Photographs by BigStockPhoto.com and Istockphoto.com
Illustrations by Allen Boe and Istockphoto.com
Design by Allen Boe

This book is available at quantity discounts for bulk purchases.
For information, please call 1-800-289-0963.

# FORBIDDEN KNOWLEDGE TRAVEL

# INTRODUCTION:

There are lots of travel books that tell you how to do stuff that you really should know how to do, like exchange currency or rent a car. But have you ever wondered about the things that you really should NOT know how to do, like talk your way past a border guard, crash a nude beach, protect against a tiger attack, or pick up a ladyboy in Bangkok?

Do you know how to smoke on an airplane without getting caught, how to go about finding a lost Amazonian tribe, how to join an anti-whaling crew, sneak into Mecca, or buy a human kidney in the Philippines? Now we're not suggesting that you go out and start being a riotous menace, but that doesn't stop you from being curious about how it's done, right? This book has been written in the same spirit as one might sell a pimp suit to a priest—the information will pique your curiosity, but we hope that you'll never have occasion to use it.

In this outrageous handbook, 101 travel related activities are road tested, from the ridiculous to the downright illegal. Many are country-specific; some are culinary; others will get you arrested, injured, or infected wherever you are in the world. This book doesn't just go to the edge—it takes you on a white-knuckle ride right along the edge without stopping for pee breaks to experience thrills that are so out there that the beaten path will become a distant memory.

## NOTICE: TO ALL CONCERNED

00567822

# CONTENTS

# 1. Pretend to Be Blind:

Pretending to be bereft of sight is a precious asset for any unscrupulous traveler. From the moment you board the crowded airport bus (kick the old lady out of her seat—your needs are greater than hers) and spend the entire journey leering at your fellow passengers behind your dark glasses, to the flight boarding requirements (first on, first off), there are myriad opportunities to receive favorable treatment.

## Checking In

At the check-in when your luggage is 5lbs overweight, explain that your Perkins Braille embossing machine is a heavy but essential travel aid. They won't bother to search your bag to find it. If they do and discover your stash of drugs, explain that you are blind and didn't pack the case yourself, and that someone else must have stuffed your teddy bear with eight cocaine-filled condoms.

## Touching the Pretty People

Have you noticed how most of the attractive people in the world live abroad? When you're on vacation it's hard to avoid staring at all the talent. However, if you are blind you get to bump into, grope, and fondle whoever you're attracted to. It's OK for you to do this because you are blind. How often do you see a blind person getting slapped for inappropriate behavior? Almost never, so enjoy. There are also more spoiled children overseas. Step on them frequently.

## Potty Time

Toilets abroad (especially in France) are best avoided, and peeing in the restroom sink is always preferable to squatting over some stinking hole in the floor. It's OK for you to do this because you are blind.

## Keeping It Real

You'll get offered lots of free tickets or the best seats in restaurants and at tourist attractions out of misguided pity, and you'll always be bumped up to first class when you fly. If anyone begins to suspect that you are faking, draw their attention to your seeing-eye dog. That should shut them up. The animal can travel with you anywhere for free and can even come in cabin with you. If you don't own a dog, then you'll have to rely on a convincing appearance—before you embark.

# 2. Get a Fake Passport:

Securing a fake passport in Europe is as easy as buying a rack of automatic weapons in a 7-Eleven back home. Approach anyone on the streets and ask for directions to the nearest fake ID provider. Even if they aren't personally involved in counterfeiting they are sure to know someone who is.

## Quality Goods

Large numbers of forged passports are available on the streets of countries like England, flooding there in staggering quantities from passport "factories" in Eastern Europe and Nigeria. If you're looking for real quality, then head for Bulgaria, which as well as offering popular summer beaches and mountain ski resorts, produces some of the highest quality passport fakes in the world. Czech passports are well worth checking out too.

## Cheap and Realistic

Whichever country you choose for fake citizenship, you'll find cheap and realistic products and you may even be able to negotiate a healthy discount when you buy in bulk. Hand over a wad of unmarked bills to a middle man (or woman), along with three recent passport photos, your height, age, and your new identity, and your documents will find their way to you quicker than you can say Shanghai Surprise. While we're on the subject of the Far East, Thailand has recently emerged as the world capital for fake passports tailored to the terrorist and criminal communities. However, don't bother going there, since up to 90 percent of the fakes are bound for Europe anyway. Fortunately even the British Home Office can't recognize a forgery even when it is under their nose. Recently a fake passport sent to them for verification was returned to an illegal immigrant without being detected.

Another option is to ask the International Red Cross to grant you a *laissez-passer* passport; rumor has it that their administrative procedures have little changed since they gave one to top Nazi Adolf Eichmann for his retirement in Argentina.

Once you've got your fake ID you can use it for identity theft, age deception, or organized crime. However, if you want to reduce your risk of being detected, choose the country with the most shambolic border controls, which is . . . you guessed it, the UK. As long as you look smart and confident, and don't bring too many bags with you, you'll be welcomed with open borders. However, when you fly home be warned that the UK charges obscenely high Air Passenger Duty (APD). How else can the government claw back money lost to the black economy through inept security arrangements?

# 3. Join an Anti-Whaling Crew:

The roar of the waves, the thrill of the catch; the air is thick with the shrill cries of seamen as they face off against each other in a battle over the world's largest marine mammals. Roaming around the freezing seas of the North Pacific are vessels staffed with men armed with harpoons on the quest for a dwindling source of lipstick and protein. Chasing after them are speedy ships manned by animal-loving activists looking to put their boats between Ahab and Moby. Go on the high-seas adventure of your life and join the crew (that's protecting Moby, of course).

## Do Your Research

If you think you've missed your vocation but don't know where to begin, you're never too old to start saving whales. However, as any career counselor will tell you, you'll need to do your research. So, if you haven't seen *The Perfect Storm* or *Free Willy* before, rent them on DVD pronto. You need to know what you're getting into when it comes to dangerous sailing conditions, and having a little boy's spirit to save a whale.

## Understand Your Enemies

The majority of whaling crews hail from Japan. However, contrary to popular belief, the Japanese attitude to hunting isn't as profligate as it first appears. It was the Norwegians who introduced whale killing on a biblical scale at a time when Japanese fishermen regarded whales as gods of the seas, albeit tasty ones.

An international moratorium on whale hunting has been in force since 1986, but Japan is allowed to kill around a thousand whales each year for research purposes. They don't want to kill Willy to eat him. They just want to kill him, cut him up into a thousand little pieces, and study him.

## Understand Your Crew

If you are serious about heading out on open water to stop the slaughter of the ocean's gentle giants, look into joining the ranks of the Sea Shepherd Conservation Society. This non-profit sails out of Washington state as well as Melbourne, Australia, and was featured on the Animal Planet's *Whale Wars*.

The goal of Sea Shepherd is to protect endangered marine mammals like whales, dolphins, and seals. They go about their conservation efforts by conducting non-violent assaults on whaling boats, both at sea and on the docks. A favored tactic is "stink-bombing" the ships with butyric acid, which they like to describe as "basically rancid butter." So pack up those sticks of butter that have been sitting in the back of your fridge since '98 and go out and eighty-six those whalers.

# 4. Get Bumped Up to First Class:

On an airplane the comfort gap between First Class and coach is enough to make you chew your polyester seat with envy: delicious foods, personal HD TV, more leg room than the Boston Celtics bench, plus you avoid lowlifes like you. There are health benefits too: on a long haul flight you'll need some quality sleep and want to reduce the risk of getting a deep vein thrombosis. So how do you get bumped up to First?

1. Getting anything for nothing is always a matter of psychology and how you deal with human beings, because they sit between you and comfort. First of all, you've got to look like you belong in First Class, so wear a suit, look clean and well-groomed, and act confident (but not brash). The other flyers have paid a lot of money to avoid scruffy backpackers, children, and other forms of pond life, so you won't stand a chance of upgrading if you look like you belong with the sweating masses.

2. If you have frequent flyer status then you will have priority over other coach-class customers. Failing this,

make sure you look like a seasoned traveler rather than a newbie looking for a freebie.

3. Pick the right moment. Usually if there are some upgrades happening, they are awarded to those frequent flyers who checked in first, but equally, if you check in last the ticket counter agent will have a better idea of how many free First Class seats are available or unclaimed.

4. If the flight is oversold, offer to be bumped on to the next flight. If the airline can't get you on another flight within an hour, you'll get a free ride. And they will look favorably on you if any First Class seats come up for grabs.

5. When booking explain that you are a famous travel writer, and ask for an OSI code to be added to your record. At the check-in hold your doctored copy of an influential travel guide (with your name prominently displayed on the spine and front cover), and explain your requirements. Most airlines will bend over backwards to ensure you give them a favorable report.

6. Don't use the word "upgrade." It's too pushy and clumsy. Be a little more sophisticated by enquiring if you can have a seat close to the front, or one with more leg room.

7. Cause a problem with your seat. Damage the safety belt, smear excrement on the food shelf, or crush some peanuts on your seat and then explain to the flight attendant that you are allergic to nuts and will go into anaphylactic shock unless you are moved to a First Class seat where you can be absolutely certain that you won't be exposed to any more nut-based hazards. If they don't believe you, show them your adrenalin pump and tracheotomy scar (this requires prior preparation).

8. You can also get moved if you have a legitimate complaint against a neighboring passenger. If he is a man, complain that he keeps pressing himself against you and staring at your genitals.

If all else fails, fake your own death shortly after take off. It is standard practice for corpses to be moved to First Class where there is more space, but choose your airline carefully: some carriers such as Singapore Airlines have introduced "corpse cupboards" to stow the recently deceased, so you might find yourself being unceremoniously stuffed into one of the cabin crew's personal lockers.

# 5. Crash a Nude Beach:

As long as you don't mind appearing naked, there's really no need to "crash" a nude beach, since all you have to do is turn up minus your clothes and off you go. However, there are some things you should know in order to blend in and to minimize the risk of being thrown off.

## Eyes Down

The most important rule is that nudists don't like to be stared at. Now we know that sounds a bit weird, right? They take off all their clothes, or play volleyball to get all their wobbly parts moving, and then they become indignant when you stroll past with your hands in your pockets and a rack of cameras around your neck. Psychologists of counter culture have a word for this: hypocrisy. You'll find a lot of it in nudist circles. People often make decisions based on their emotions, which can be notoriously flaky at the best of times. In this case, their emotions tell them that walking around butt naked is natural, when in fact they should listen to their brains warning them that someone else might find this quite arousing and want to take home several memory-aids.

## Wear Yourself Out

The other no-no is sexual activity. Yes, it just doesn't make sense, but apparently the nudity is totally non-sexual, mainly because most of the men have masturbated themselves stupid before breakfast. If you're a man it's the only guarantee of reducing the risk of getting a boner on the beach, which is another taboo.

## So Much for Freedom

There's so much to think about that you may find the whole operation too stressful. Oh, and don't forget to bring a towel. You'll need it to lie on and to cover up when you visit communal areas, such as the toilet, parking lot, or beach café. Drape it on chairs before sitting to avoid leaving butt stains—another worry. Respect the beach, and help control litter. Always bring a trash bag for your own litter, and take your used tissues home with you.

People visit nudist beaches for a number of reasons, but since the main motivation is exhibitionism or gawking behind a façade of studied nonchalance, relax—they are not so different from you after all.

# 6. Become a Snake Charmer:

What about snake charming doesn't sound like a great idea? Sitting inches away from a poisonous snake, taunting it with obnoxious flute music, having it rise into striking position . . . it sounds awesome! If you're interested in learning the tricks of the trade, you should head over to India where the modern concept of snake charming originated.

## What's the Charm?

Once seen as a national treasure—snake charmers were flown around the world to promote tourism to India—the practice is now technically outlawed; however, you can still find practitioners throughout the country, playing their instruments and making their serpents wiggle and rise from their baskets.

Snake charmers set up shop like other types of street performers. They try and find a heavily trafficked area and claim a spot where they can set their basket and begin playing their *been* or *pungi*, the flute-like instrument favored by charmers. As the charmers play their music, the snake—usually a cobra or viper—rises from the basket and waves in the air as if entranced by the music. In actuality, the snake cannot hear the music, but can feel the vibrations. Also, it is not hypnotized; it is just getting into a defensive position in order to strike.

## Where to Begin

First things first, if you want to be a snake charmer, you need a snake. You could go out in the Indian wild and try your luck at capturing a cobra. Chances are you will wind up getting bitten. Therefore, you should head to a local gift store and purchase the realest looking, fake snake that you can find. Trust us, this is much safer.

## Snake in the Grass

Seeing as how your fake snake will not be reacting to the vibrations put out by your flute, you are going to need to get creative. After you purchase an authentic Indian basket, you will need to buy some extra-fine fishing line. Next, find a place to set up your scam that has some sort of overhang. A street light or building's eave should work. You need to tie the line around your snake's head, loop it over the overhang, and tie it around your flute. Once you take the top off your basket, begin playing your flute, twisting the instrument clockwise as you play. This will reel the line around the flute and raise your snake. Be sure to move the flute around as it will not only make your snake "dance" but it will distract your onlookers. When the snake reaches its peak height, begin twisting the flute counter-clockwise in order to put your snake to bed.

# 7. Stow Away on Board a Ship:

A stowaway is anyone who hides on a train, bus, plane, ship, or bicycle in the hope of getting something for nothing, or moving from one country to another illegally. As most sensible people know, you get what you pay for, and when you become a stowaway, you expose yourself to considerable danger and discomfort. There are also serious legal consequences if you are discovered, especially on a plane. If you get caught you will most likely be treated as a terrorist and get hauled off to Cuba for some heavy-duty waterboarding.

## Freight with Danger

Each form of transport comes with its own risks. Every year lots of people are injured trying to jump off moving trains, while airplane stowaways are often found frozen to death inside the landing gear. The major hazard for ship stowaways is choosing the wrong hold and being crushed by millions of tons of cargo, or being unprepared for the length of the trip. Be ready for many weeks at sea; be sure to have adequate supplies of food and water you will be dead within a few days. That said, there is a certain romantic appeal to placing your fate in the hands of a crew of jolly jack tars as they sail their trade through the high seas.

The safest vessel on which to hitch a lift is a container ship, as they have low levels of security and more places to hide, especially empty containers. The port and starboard service tunnels which run below decks are good places to board.

## Longshoremen

Many stowaways have successfully posed as dock laborers by dressing up like Marlon Brando in On the Waterfront. If you don't own a leather jacket, then a hard hat, jeans, and an orange visibility jacket will suffice. When lifting, always bend your knees and keep your back straight, otherwise everyone will quickly spot an impostor. Also, learn a few knots, because you may be asked to throw together a Square Knot Bracelet to prove your credentials. Bone up on a few nautical terms before your trip, so that if you are challenged you can slap your thigh and speak authentically: "Arr, listen close me hearty, I be no landlubber by the powers, as ye soon shall see mateys, or ye can call me a scurvy dog!" As the gulls wheel overhead, hand them back the knotted rope with a toothless grin and, with a glint in your good eye, offer to buy them a quart of grog.

# 8. Be a Sex Tourist:

The international tourism industry is booming and the sex industry is ever burgeoning as air travel becomes cheaper and cheaper. If you want to spend your vacation dollars wisely, then you can do no better than boost the economy of a third world country. Instead of offering hand-outs, you'll be paying for a service which gives its impoverished participants dignity and the prospect of a better life.

## Saving Lives

It goes without saying that the best place to exploit people for sex is in poor countries where you can offer financial incentives in exchange for tricks. When someone is on the bread line, not only does your money help to boost the economy, it also literally saves lives. The most significant societal factor that pushes people into prostitution is poverty, so the only responsible thing is for the more fortunate among us to do whatever we can to alleviate their suffering. Poverty also correlates with illiteracy, so you can have the added satisfaction of knowing that you are helping to educate as well.

## Better the Devil You Know

Oftentimes, women are lured to the cities with hopes of finding work. They rely on your money when those jobs fail to materialize. Many prostitutes live in constant fear of being beaten up by clients or by pimps, or being arrested by the police. At least you know that when you show them a little kindness and financial assistance, it's one less reason for them to take risks or feel depressed.

## Where to Go

Now that we've made the case for sex tourism, we just have to point you in the right direction. Between 2 and 14 percent of the gross domestic product of Indonesia, Malaysia, the Philippines, and Thailand comes from sex tourism, but if you are worried about your carbon footprint when you fly half way around the world to avoid the laws in your own country, then go to closer-to-home locations like Mexico and Central America, which have much to satisfy the libido of the wary traveler.

# 9. Con Your Way into the Space Program:

If you dream of an exciting career that combines peeing in a bag with floating around a freezing vacuum, look no further than the space program. Aim for the stars! Not all astronauts are geniuses with IQs of 160; some are muscular jet pilots as well. However, some programs are easier to get into than others.

## It Ain't Rocket Science

At NASA, which send shuttles up faster than Jim Carrey changes his facial expressions, you won't get past the receptionist, while over at the European Space Agency you can bribe all the security guards with a ripe Camembert and a packet of Gitanes (although it doesn't look like any of its rockets will make it into orbit until at least 2060). If you have a few hundred million to spare, you can always hitch a lift to the Space Station with the Russians.

## G-force Unit

In most space programs, before they'll let you fly a rocket (or rather, grip the steering wheel and let the G-force wreck you while two million tons of volatile propellant explodes under your seat), you either have to be a super-fit pilot with a science degree who has clocked more than a thousand hours of experience in charge of a jet airplane, or spend several more years studying to be a payload specialist (all so you can fool around with a robotic arm, a skill any child can learn on a pick-and-grab machine in the mall). You will also be expected to be cool under pressure and scribble down lots of "gimble co-ordinates" like Gary Sinise in *Apollo 13*. Even then, if you get the sniffles, or are found to be too short (below 5' 4") or too tall (above 6' 3") you'll fail the height restriction and go back to flipping burgers. Clearly you need to know an extra trick to bump you to the front of the line.

## SASPIS

Few people are aware that NASA is currently recruiting willing participants in a top-secret eugenics project called SASPIS which is jointly-funded by the CIA and the US Census Bureau. All you have to do to qualify is pass an IQ test consisting of a short presentation: a Census agent projects onto the wall in letters two-feet high the words "Send All the Stupid People into Space." When they turn on the lights and ask if you've changed your mind—here is the important part—make sure you say, "NO." Congratulations, you just won your ticket out of here, and can expect to be heading towards the Kuiper Belt within the week.

# 10. Scam Your Fellow Tourists:

Travelers have been ripping each other off ever since Moses's disastrous forty-year mystery tour. Here are three classics:

## The Airport Metal-Detector Push-In

This one is real easy, but you'll need a partner to pull it off. First your partner puts their stuff through the metal detector. You wait until the next person (your mark) has put their bag on the conveyor belt, and then you barge past him/her in a hurry, but you set off the alarm and spend ages emp-

tying your pockets of all your belongings. As the victim stands patiently waiting for you to finish, their bag has been picked up by your friend on the other side, and whipped away. If they don't let you push in front and you get involved in an argument, the end result is the same—the distraction enables your partner to make a clean getaway. In 1977 a Texan oil baroness was parted from her bag in this way; it contained more than $500,000 in jewelry.

## The Bus Insurance Scam

After you've gained the trust of some of your fellow tourists, inform them of the sure-fire insurance scam that you've got wind of. They pay $200 dollars to a fixer and they are guaranteed to get ten times that amount back. Then they get on a bus, which will get rear-ended a few miles down the road. They will be able to claim compensation by feigning whiplash injuries, so the bus company will start throwing money at them to avoid a costly litigation. They hand over the money to you and climb aboard, but when the bus reaches its destination without incident they know they've been scammed, but you are miles away (or rather, they are) and you have their cash. It sounds like an implausible stunt, but hundreds of gullible tourists have fallen for this scam.

## Fake Policeman

Share some of your dope with some of your fun-loving tourist friends, and enjoy a good booze up and spliff session on the beach. Pretend you are the worse for wear and leave the party early, but make sure that there is still plenty of illicit stash doing the rounds. This is the signal for your real friends to arrive five minutes later posing as law enforcement. They take a wad of cash in bribes, and confiscate the drugs, which you can all divvy up later.

# 11. Talk Your Way Past a Border Guard:

If you want to cross a border, the golden rule is don't cross the border guard. He stands between you and forward progress, so you have to play on his terms and stay calm, compliant and respectful, no matter what, even when you know you are being taken for a ride.

Borders can be very frustrating places, where you feel that things are out of your control, but remember that when the going gets tough you can at least control your own emotions and behavior. In many cases, your attitude dictates how you are treated. If you get impatient and start making demands, you can expect to be given the full five-star body and vehicle search, which is not a pleasant experience and can set you back hours.

# Ten Ways to Keep Your Mind and Body Together

1. Be organized. Have all your passports, visas, and other travel documents ready for presentation. Being disorganized wastes the guards' time and they will waste yours in return, plus they will judge you for your sloppiness.

2. The same goes for your appearance—look smart (but not too smart—nothing says "hit me for a bribe" better than a $2,000 suit and Rolex). Men: have a shave—scruffy equals untrustworthy—and remove your sunglasses and hat.

3. Treat everyone with respect but don't be a pushover. If you suspect that you are being asked for a bribe, pretend you don't understand and ask for a receipt. Don't assume that the guards are low in the pecking order; in some countries they are important government officials.

4. Stick together. If one of you is asked to enter the post, make sure one of your party accompanies them, but don't leave your vehicle unattended.

5. Keep your trunk tidy; an untidy trunk can be all the excuse a guard needs to strip down your vehicle. If this happens, don't wander off for a smoke; remain with your wheels and keep vigilant for light-fingered guards.

6. Stay calm and focused. Hesitation or nerves will make you look like you have something to hide.

7. Find out the busiest crossing times (such as weekends and public vacations) and avoid them, otherwise you may incur overtime fees, or be kept waiting until they become payable.

8. Now is not the time to try out any of your wisecracks. Making a joke about how much dope you've got stashed in the tires is an invitation to have them cut open. Border crossing is a serious business. By all means laugh if the guard makes a joke, but save your one-liners for later.

9. If you own expensive equipment (wristwatch, camera, etc.) that looks new, carry a photocopy of the purchase receipt, otherwise it will be hard to prove that you aren't smuggling goods in or out of the country.

10. Don't stare. The guards may be carrying some neat looking automatic weapons, but if you eyeball them too much, they will get twitchy and suspicious.

# 12. Go Over Niagara Falls in a Barrel:

And chance coming back in a box. Sixteen people have attempted the stunt and eleven have survived (two men have done it twice and lived). That's good odds, considering that Horseshoe Falls has a vertical drop of 170 feet (52 meters). No matter the materials you use for your "barrel" and how meticulous the planning, the stunt is still very dangerous so here's a quick checklist as you make your plans in the bar.

1. Avoid the American Falls, as there are too many rocks at the bottom. All successful attempts have been over the Horseshoe Falls (unfortunately this does require a trip over the border to Canada).

2. Despite the success rate, there have been some nasty injuries, such as those of Bobby Leach (the first person to use a steel barrel, way back in 1911). He broke his jaw and both kneecaps and spent six months in the hospital. Can you afford to be out of work for that long?

3. The main hazard is that the barrel will hit rocks and split open and then you'll either drown or get your body smashed by the water and the rocks. Most modern attempts have used materials such as rubber and metal, sometimes both. Experience shows that your barrel should be light and strong. In 1984, Karel Soucek used lightweight wood

and plastic, and some ballast in the bottom ensured he descended feet-first. However, if your container is too flimsy, like "The Thing" used by William "Red" Hill Jr. in 1951, it may survive the fall but break apart under the cascade of water. He died. In 1920, Charles Stevens (the third person to attempt it) strapped himself inside a very heavy oak barrel and tied an anvil to his feet for ballast. Don't do this. The anvil smashed through the bottom of the barrel taking him with it, leaving behind one of his arms. He also died.

4. Wood is good but rubber is better. In 1928, Jean Lussier used a six-foot rubber ball with thirty-two inner tubes reinforced with steel bands. He survived unharmed. Thirty-three years later, Nathan Boya used a steel sphere encased in six-ply rubber with similar results. Probably the best design was used in Steve Trotter's and Lori Martin's second successful attempt in 1995: two hot water tanks, surrounded by a thick layer of Kevlar; it was also the most expensive option, costing $19,000.

5. Take some sandwiches and air tanks, so you don't get hungry or suffocate waiting to be rescued. In 1930, George Stathakis suffocated after getting stuck behind the water curtain for 18 hours (his companion, a pet turtle, survived).

6. Even if you survive you will be fined up to a maximum of $10,000 plus court costs for "stunting without a license." (In 1995, Steve Trotter also spent 2 weeks in jail.)

Do it for the thrill but not for the fame. Before today, did you know the names of anyone who has gone before? Maybe the sixty-three-year-old retired school teacher Annie Edson Taylor who was the first person to attempt it (with her cat) in 1901, using a modified pickle barrel. But it didn't gain her the wealth and notoriety she so badly craved, and she died two decades later, broke. Plus her cat never forgave her.

# 13. Have Underground Cosmetic Surgery in Brazil:

Plastic surgery tourism offers a vacation that pays for itself; you can recoup the cost by what you save in health care while enjoying an exotic vacation where you can pick up some unique souvenirs and leave your worries at Rio de Janeiro airport along with ten pounds of tummy fat on the return journey. Besides, it's got to be better booking two weeks abroad than to have to tell your boss you're having liposuction.

Where else can you enjoy sun, fun, and surgery at bargain basement prices (apart from Malaysia, Thailand, South Africa, Costa Rica, or the Philippines)? Brazil proudly receives clients from all over the world seeking the cheapest plastic surgeons this side of Kuala Lumpur. The country is famous for its stunning women and its international soccer players, so it is the natural place to experience body modification.

## Quick Hands for Such a Big Fella

Most surgeons are licensed by the Brazilian Football Con-
federation (CBF) and they are currently ranked fifth by FIFA for
buttock implants, liposculpture, and taking a dive in the penalty area. You can go under the knife confident in the knowledge
that you are in the capable hands of doctors who serve five-time
World Cup winners. All the doctors are mono-lingual, so that if
you wake up paralysed on the operating table just blink your
eyes rapidly to attract their attention and to let them know
that you would like some more anaesthetic.

## Take the Shot

As you would expect from a bustling South American capital, crime is a normal part of everyday life and no areas of
the city or times of day are immune, but if you get shot here
you'll be stitched up for a third of the price. However, make
sure you remove all jewelry and other valuables from your
person before the operation as an unconscious patient always
attracts the attention of thieves.

## What a Clinical Finish

The best time to visit is four days before Ash Wednesday;
that way you can enjoy Carnival and then have surgery, leaving you plenty of R&R time before you fly home. Each procedure
comes with a some-of-your-money-back guarantee that nearly
all of the scars will be almost invisible to the naked eye at
thirty paces.

# 14. Pick Up a Ladyboy in Bangkok:

The most difficult part of picking up a ladyboy is spotting one. Then all you have to do when she opens the transaction with "Hello, very cheap-cheap," is buy her a drink and show you're looking to add to your already impressive collection of STDs. Here's how to pick a ladyboy out from a gaggle of gorgeous Thai girls.

1. She's the one with the five o'clock shadow. Here's a clue: Thai girls don't shave their faces, so if you see any indication of facial hair you're in luck. She may try to hide it with make up (Thai girls don't wear very much so the more make up, the greater then chance you've got a guy). Anyway, it will be so humid that she'll probably sweat away most of her foundation so you can get a proper look at her lovely stubble.

2. The more gorgeous she is, the greater the odds that she's sporting a penis. If she's a girl, then what the hell is she doing in this seedy bar talking to you when she could be making her fortune modeling or dating a millionaire? If

she looks too perfect, then she's probably been surgically enhanced, which means she's also got boy tackle.

3. She carries a roll of duct tape in her handbag. How else is she going to strap it out of sight?

4. Check out her neck. If you can see an Adam's apple, she's a dude.

5. Thai girls are generally short and very feminine. If your date is tall and has good muscle definition, you've hit the jackpot (although she may simply be Cambodian).

6. Look at her extremities: Thai girls tend not to wear size eleven heels and are generally incapable of carrying three pints of lager with one hand.

7. Check out her friends. If she is hanging around with ugly Betties who are quite clearly ladyboys, then she is probably one too (but she's the best of the bunch, so stick around).

8. When you get back to your hotel room she will insist on turning off the lights, or encourage you to do her from behind.

9. If you can't stand the suspense any longer, have a grope or just cut to the chase and ask her, "Are you a ladyboy?"

# 15. Sneak into Mecca:

Mecca is in Saudi Arabia and is Islam's holiest city. It is the birthplace of the prophet Muhammad, the founder of the Islamic faith, and the place towards which Muslims around the globe face five times daily when they pray. Only Muslims are allowed into Mecca (as well as Islam's other holy city, Medina, the burial place of Muhammad, 210 miles northwest). Any non-Muslims caught in either city face dire consequences, either execution by the Saudi authorities, or even spontaneous death at the hands of an angry mob.

## Book Burning

You may think this is unfair and retrograde, since the holy cities of Jerusalem and Rome are open to all, regardless of their religion, and you'd be right, but you have been warned and we in no way encourage you to do this. If you do, leave this book at home. Seriously. In fact, burn it: the last thing anyone needs right now is another Fatwah. Also, it's best to avoid the week of Hajj (the 8th to 12th day of *Dhu al-Hijjah*, the 12th month of the Islamic calendar), unless you want to become one of the hundreds of devout pilgrims who are trampled to death each year in the religious mayhem.

## Infidel Explorers

A handful of infidel explorers have traveled in secret to Mecca and lived to tell the tale; the most famous was Sir Richard Burton who published *Personal Narrative of a Pilgrimage to al-Madinah & Meccah* in 1855 and claimed to be the "only living European who has found his way to the Head Quarters of the Muslim Faith." He went deep undercover, living as a dervish (a Sufi mendicant ascetic) in Sind and studied every aspect of Muslim culture, even apprenticing himself to a blacksmith to learn how to make horseshoes.

## Grow a Beard

You don't have to go to these extremes. If you come from a country like the US where religion does not appear on your passport, then in theory you should just need to grow a beard, wear a cream-colored *abaya* (or *hijab* if you are female), and gain some knowledge of Islam so you know which way to walk (counter-clockwise) around a large black cube called the Ka'bah, Islam's most sacred monument, and when to lower your head to the ground in prayer.

## Mosque-See

When you arrive in Mecca, unload your luggage at the hotel and go straight to the Grand Mosque (Masjid al-Haram). Make sure you enter with the right foot first and keep your gaze lowered until you have a clear view of the Ka'bah. Then place your hands together and start praying. When you get home tell nobody what you've done, and definitely don't write a book about it.

# 16. Fly for Free:

Imagine if you could fly anywhere in the world free of charge, with no boarding lines and no hassle. Well, imagine you're a world leader or an airline pilot then because for most of us there's no such thing as a free lunch. Or is there?

## Get Born on a Plane

Being born on a plane used to guarantee free air travel for life; it's less likely these days because no airline allows passengers to fly if they are more than thirty-two weeks pregnant without a doctor's note, and not at all beyond thirty-six weeks. In any case, that was largely an urban myth, since there have only been two recorded incidents of a baby being awarded free flights for life. This is the exception, not the rule. Anyway, that's no good for you because you've already been born.

## Get Bumped

Every day hundreds of people get free plane tickets from major airlines. These people agree to be bumped onto a later flight when too many passenger turn up for the scheduled flight (all flights are generally overbooked by 10 percent, to allow for no-shows). If the airline can't find you another flight leaving within the hour, then you will get at least $500 off your next flight, plus a coupon for about $100. Just before boarding, the airline will make an announcement asking if anyone agrees to step off. Make sure you have flexible travel arrangements so you can take advantage of the offer. Increase your chances further by volunteering to get bumped when you first check in.

## Collect Air Miles on Your Credit Card

Lots of credit cards offer air miles for every dollar that you spend on the card. If you spend a gazillion dollars on your credit card you'll get a free ticket. However, be warned that some of these cards have very high interest rates (as high as 50 percent), so make sure you set up a direct debit to pay off the balance every month without fail to avoid any interest. Many stores also do loyalty cards that offer air miles.

## Date a Pilot or Flight Attendant

Airline crews have a quota of free tickets for themselves and their family. Don't get married though, because you'll spend evenings alone, eating pizza in front of endless reruns of *CSI*, while your partner flies around the world. Pay attention—that's the exact opposite of what we're trying to achieve here!

## Pretend to Have Cancer

That's more like it. There are several organizations that pay for flights for people to travel to their cancer treatment such as the Air Charity Network, or the Corporate Angel Network, to name but two. Shave your hair off and jump on the gravy plane. If you want to keep your hair, Lifeline Pilots caters to other illnesses too.

## Become an Air Courier

Becoming an air courier is very easy. You just have to dress well and collect a parcel from the airline, and deliver it safely to your destination. Join the International Association of Air Travel Couriers (IAATC) and have a clean passport. Most carriers allow only one courier per flight, so two of you wouldn't be able to travel this way for free.

## Mail Yourself

Get a friend to duct tape you into a sturdy box, and ship you to your destination by air freight. Take plenty of bottled water (drink the water and pee in the empty bottles) and wrap up warm because temperatures in the hold will reach well below zero.

# 17. Increase Your Carbon Footprint:

What's the big deal about global warming? It isn't going to kill the planet; just the human race, and who are we to think that we are any more important than all the other species that have lived, 95 percent of which are now extinct? The main function of the threat of global warming is a political stick to beat up developing countries like China so we can berate them for becoming the next global superpower.

## Unwelcome Impressions

Even the name "carbon footprint" is emotive and misleading, since it throws up images of unwelcome impressions left in moist concrete or tiny animals being crushed under foot. A better term would be "carbon cup size." At least this would allow people to compare their alleged impact on the planet in a graphically humorous way, and one to which our image-obsessed culture can actually relate.

## Hit and Myth

The dinosaurs lasted for millions of years longer than we ever will, and yet our creation myths encourage us to view ourselves as the pinnacle to which all life aspires. Once you free yourself from this vain and human-centric world view, you will see that far from reducing your carbon footprint, you should increase it. Besides, the combined bio-mass of ants creates more greenhouse gases than humans, but they don't worry themselves about it. "Smug" (a deadly greenhouse gas produced by Prius drivers and other eco do-gooders as detailed in *South Park*) is a bigger threat to society than $CO_2$.

## Up the Garden Path

OK, so the first thing you need to stop doing is gardening. Did you know that if you plant six trees each year, you will completely offset the emissions of your Hummer? And stop washing your clothes in lukewarm water already. Despite what it says on the television, modern washing detergents do NOT get stains out at low temperatures. We all know this, but instead of complaining we keep quiet and become complicit in this mass deception. The exponentially low wash temperatures on clothing care labels prove that manufacturers know that their increasingly shoddy goods will disintegrate in hot water. Fifty years ago you could boil all your clothes in a twin tub with no ill effects. So go back to washing at 70 degrees and use your consumer power to demand better quality fabrics.

## An Appeal to Reason

Stop feeling guilty people. We urge you in the strongest possible terms to read *An Appeal to Reason* in which Nigel Lawson takes a cool look at global warming. When you've finished reading it, take a road trip to a friend's house so you can burn some more gas and personally deliver some common sense. The sooner we use up so-called dwindling supplies of oil (Peak-Oil is another myth, by the way), the quicker we can withdraw troops from Iraq, and go back to ignoring Canada. You know it makes sense.

# 18. Live in an Airport:

Tom Hanks did it in *The Terminal*, and a German woman called Bettina has spent the last decade living in Palma's main terminal in Majorca with her white cat Mumu and a bunch of suitcases. Spain is good like that. It's the living-in-an-airport capital of the world, where the authorities usually turn a blind eye. Staying alive is the easy bit; keeping your marbles is a different matter.

Don't bother trying to take up residence in an airport in the UK. It is estimated that there are about 100 people living in Heathrow at any given time (and approximately twenty in Gatwick), but it won't be long before you are issued with an Anti-Social Behavior Order (ASBO) and get tossed out.

## Head in the Crowds

It's easy to blend in with the other travelers for a few days, even weeks, since there are always lots of people waiting for delayed flights, and it's got to be better than living on the streets. For starters, you are less likely to get beaten up in an airport, with security cameras everywhere and armed police just a shout away. It's big, it's centrally heated, and it's free. No taxes, no bills, no rent. Why doesn't everyone live in an airport?

Be prepared though: hard fluorescent lights beat down their watts relentlessly 24-7. Get yourself a good face mask for sleeping, and ear plugs to shut out the annoying announcements. During the day, try to look like you belong: wear business attire and talk loudly into your cell phone, or go casual and carry a large souvenir like a piñata. Look bored—after day two that shouldn't be too hard.

## Fine Dining

Begging will get you thrown out. Arcade games, vending machines, and a quick search of the cushions of any chair may reward you with a few neglected coins. If you can find the change for a Big Mac Meal, you've nailed most of your caloric requirements for the day. Otherwise, make like a pigeon and swoop in on the many half-eaten meals abandoned by tardy travelers.

## Lonely Days

Human company is probably the biggest thing you'll miss. You'll easily strike up a conversation during the first few weeks, but as your poor diet, lack of sleep, and hygiene deteriorate, most people will give you a wide berth. Your loneliness will be magnified by your proximity to crowds. Also, there's no point being territorial—everyone likes their own space, but here everything and nothing belongs to you.

# 19. Run with the Bulls in Pamplona:

Each year between July 6th and 14th, the Spanish town of Pamplona hosts celebrations for the Festival of San Fermin, better known as the Pamplona Bull Running. The mayor stands on the balcony of the Casa Consistorial and declares the festival officially open to the watching crowd assembled in the square below. A rocket is let off. It's all very civilized. The mental stuff begins the following morning.

## The Route

The route runs for half a mile from the corral and ends at the great stadium of the Plaza del Toros, where the bulls are penned in again. The streets along the route are fenced off so the bulls can't escape. At 8 A.M., six killer bulls are released as well as two herds of castrated bulls, or steers. With uncharacteristic understatement, the Spanish call the event *El Encierro* (the enclosing).

## Mental and Physical Preparation

Stay up drinking the night before, so that you are still drunk in the morning, but don't be so legless you can't walk or the police will stop you from running. Dress in the traditional costume of the bull runner: white shirt and pants (baggy cotton or linen that allows plenty of freedom of movement), red belt, and tie a red handkerchief around your neck.

Assemble bright and early beneath the great cathedral in the center of town with all the other intoxicated Mediterranean bucks as you decide where to begin your run. The first leg of the route—the Passage of Santo Domingo—is the most dangerous, because the bulls', legs and lungs are fresh and the course is uphill. Only the bravest and the most stupid runners attempt this. The middle part of the run, the *Ayuntamiento* is the widest and safest. It begins at the end of Santo Domingo and ends at the first corner of La Estafeta, where the streets narrow again. Another very dangerous part of the route is the downward curve into Duque de Ahumada (also known as the Telefónica stretch). The last bit of the route is also very dangerous where it leads into the stadium.

## Ready, Steady, Bleed

At 8 A.M., a rocket shooting into the cloudless sky signals that the corral gate has been opened. At this point it is customary to utter a short prayer to Saint Fermin before you start running for your life. A second rocket indicates that the bulls have left the corral and that they are pissed. The rest needs little explanation in the same way that distancing

yourself from a large hairy sociopath waving a bloody cleaver
needs no pointers.

Try to blend into the herd. A lone bull is very dangerous,
but if you can run along with two or more bulls, they will
gore the stragglers they come upon and leave you alone, allegedly. If you fall over, you're in trouble because you will get
gored and trampled by bulls and runners in front of thousands
of cheering spectators.

After two-and-a-half minutes that seem like an hour, a third
rocket indicates that the bulls have entered the bullring, and
a fourth rocket tells you that the bulls are safely locked up
in the bull pen, whereupon you can lie down exhausted on the
ancient cobbled street and bleed out in peace.

# 20. Eat First and Ask Questions Later:

Want to feel a thrill that will hit you right in the pit of your stomach—literally? Venture off to foreign locales and order up the country specialty, from the menu, with no translation, and no idea what you're eating. Don't ask and the chef won't tell. You could be eating an indigenous root, or you could be eating . . . it doesn't matter! You bragged to everyone how you were going to immerse yourself in the local culture, so eat up.

## Chapulines

If you head south of the border and are looking for something tasty to snack on with your *cervezas*, order up a bowl of crispy *chapulines*. See if you and your buddies can figure out what's behind the tasty treat's unfamiliar crunch. A Mexican delicacy, these bite-size delights pack a taste that's sour, salty, *and* spicy. It's a culinary adventure for your mouth. So hop to it and try them out.

## Balut

As you're walking down the crowded streets of Southeast Asia—be it in Cambodia, Vietnam, or Laos—stop at a vendor's cart and see if he has any *balut*. Chances are, he does. And if he doesn't, the guy next to him most likely does. Balut is a popular vendor food in these countries, like the hot dog is in the States. And like a hot dog, you don't want to know what you're really eating. When he hands you a small packet of salt and what resembles a hard-boiled egg, pour on the salt and start snacking. Note: you are not eating a hard-boiled egg.

## Soup No. 5

If you want to know what you're dipping in to, it's no soup for you. Next time you take off to the Philippines, start your evening meal with a big bowl of Soup No. 5. Like the Chanel perfume, it has it's own distinct aroma. Unlike the Chanel perfume, it's made of . . . now wait, that'd be cheating. Be bullish and try it for yourself. If you can nail down the ingredients, consider sending the list over to Chanel—they're always looking for a new scent.

## Betute Tugak

While you're there, why not follow your soup with an entrée of *betute tugak*? A delicacy in the Philippines, this tasty treat packs double the flavor as it is one thing stuffed with another. The French have chicken cordon bleu (chicken stuffed with ham), Americans have turducken (turkey stuffed with chicken stuffed with duck), and Filipinos have betute tugak (you almost got us).

# 21. Smoke in an Airplane:

Ah, the days when everyone smoked in-flight, and when airlines even gave you complimentary mini-packs of cigarettes on your meal trays. Those times are long gone, although a few international flights allow smoking in designated areas.

## Expensive Habit

If you're a heavy smoker and you go crazy on a long-haul flight (or a short-haul for that matter), then you need to learn how to have a cigarette in an airplane bathroom without out setting off the alarms. If you get caught, you face a $5,000 dollar fine. That's still cheaper than some of the finest Cuban cigars, but worse value than chartering your own plane. As if that wasn't enough, the FAA will send a letter asking you to explain exactly why you were smoking in the plane. Isn't it obvious? You didn't follow the following advice . . .

# No Smoke without Duct Tape

It's easy to disable the smoke alarm. Place some duct tape over the air vents, or cover it in Saran wrap and secure it with a rubber band. If the detector can't detect smoke, it can't make a noise. Don't try to unplug the detector because this will set it off. If that happens, the game is up, so come out of the stall when asked. Don't try to tough it out because the flight attendants are trained to smash in the door with a fire extinguisher at the first sign of trouble, and sometimes even when you're a little constipated.

This still leaves you with the challenge of getting rid of the smoke. It doesn't matter how nonchalantly you try to walk back to your seat, the smoke will give you away every time. The trick is to flush the toilet in between puffs using this five point plan:

1. Take a drag.

2. Remove the cigarette from your mouth so that it stays dry.

3. Stick your face as far into the bowl as you can.

4. Breathe out.

5. Flush. This eliminates the smoke and rewards you with a refreshing shower at the same time.

## Destroy the Evidence

After your last drag, do not under any circumstances throw the butt into the bowl (can't you read? PLACING OBJECTS IN TOILET MAY CAUSE SYSTEM FAILURE), or the waste paper bin. The airplane is pressurized with oxygen, so the slightest spark will cause an inferno. In any case, you should destroy the evidence: run it under the tap and then eat it. It won't do you anywhere near as much harm as a hefty fine or your three-packs-a-day habit.

# 22. Smuggle Illegal Immigrants in Your Truck :

If you are a truck driver, there's no secret to smuggling human cargo. In fact, it's easier not to, as truckers frequently face crippling fines for each immigrant that falls out of their rig when they have crossed a border. Although, many of them claim ignorance. If you can't beat them, join them, and you can use the same defense if you get caught.

## If You Can't Beat 'Em

You can make good money smuggling people from Mexico to the US (up to $10,000 each) and in Europe (at least a year's salary). Patras in Greece is one of the prime routes used by smuggling gangs from Greece to Italy, with people from as far away as Afghanistan and Iraq looking for a ride. However, recently the checking regime has stepped it up. Still, the chances are if you are doing that route anyway, you will end up with some unwanted guests, so why not make some money for the risks you are taking? This also increases the chance of you reaching your destination without having the ropes and elastic holdings slashed to pieces as the stowaways gain entry. If you get caught, your stowaways should claim political asylum; that will take some of the heat off you.

## Channel Crossing

If you are smuggling for the money rather than humanitarian purposes, you can make a fast buck on the route from France into the UK. The French will wave you through because they can't face the paperwork involved in catching illegals on their side of the Channel, especially during lunchtime. UK customs officials use sniffer dogs as well as carbon-dioxide and heartbeat detectors to catch stowaways. However, if there is something important on TV they won't search you, so try to time your journey to coincide with a soccer cup final, a royal wedding/funeral, or any Friday evening during the summer months (*Big Brother* eviction night).

## Coming Up for Air

Keep the air vents open during the transporting, and fill up with gas in case you get into a police chase. Once you arrive at your destination, hand back passports to your passengers (you remembered to confiscate them earlier, right?). Don't smuggle more than twenty-five people at a time because otherwise they could run out of air or get carbon-dioxide poisoning, and even if they all survive you'll never get rid of the smell.

# 23. Break Ridiculous Laws Abroad:

Some places like Singapore have taken the concept of the Big Brother state and really run with it, but most other nations can boast a smattering of seemingly illogical laws, or ones that have been on the statute books for so long that no one can bear to wave them goodbye.

1. Australian law forbids leaving your car keys in an unattended vehicle, giving someone a Tarot or psychic reading (which are considered forms of witchcraft), and wandering the streets wearing black clothes with your face covered in boot polish, as this is the exact attire of a cat burglar.

2. In Bahrain, a male doctor can legally examine a woman's genitals, but he must not view them directly. Instead, he must hold up a mirror and stare at the reflection.

3. When in France, you can't name your pig Napoleon, take photographs of police officers or police vehicles, and between 8 A.M. and 8 P.M., seventy percent of music on the radio must be by French artists.

4. Israel forbids the riding of bikes without a license, nose picking on the Sabbath, and feeding animals in a public place.

5. Home schooling your children in Spain is not allowed, nor is tying down the trunk of a vehicle, or listening to music with ear plugs while driving.

6. In Switzerland, you're not allowed to flush the toilet after 10 P.M., or pee standing up, and on Sundays you can't hang up laundry, or clean your car.

7. In Thailand, no one is allowed to step on the nation's currency (since it depicts the Thai Royal Family); it is also illegal to leave the house without your underwear, and you must wear a shirt while driving.

8. A married woman in Turkey can only get a job with her husband's permission, she must live where he dictates, and if they divorce all jointly-owned assets revert to him.

9. In the United Arab Emirates, belly dancing is forbidden, along with swearing or kissing in public, and it is a criminal offence to eat, drink, or smoke in public during Ramadan in daylight.

10. In the United Kingdom, it is illegal to eat mince pies on Christmas Day, or die in the Houses of Parliament, and in Scotland, if a stranger asks to use your restroom, you must let them in.

# 24. Land an Airplane in Open Water:

If you want to play the Land-an-Airbus-320-on-the-Hudson game, or any body of water for that matter, it's not as easy as it looks. Once you've lost both engines, the only chance you've got of walking away alive is to get the nose down and glide so that when you hit the water the wings are producing very little lift while your forward motion is as slow as possible in order to pull off a low-speed, low-impact landing.

## Gliding by the Seat of Your Pants

It might not surprise you to learn that airliners are not designed for gliding. A typical glider has a glide ratio of 30 or 60 to 1 which means that for every mile of altitude it can travel for 30 or 60 miles before it lands. An Airbus 320 has a fraction of that. If you lose power at 5,000 feet, you'll have about four or five minutes to land, so you've got to think really fast.

Here's what to do:

1. Send a mayday call to air traffic control and inform them that you intend to land in the water.

2. Tell the cabin crew and passengers to prepare for a crash landing.

3. Keep the landing gear stowed to make the bottom of the plane more like the hull of a boat. This will aid a smooth landing, and stops warning sirens from going off as the plane gets closer to the ground.

4. Turn off the air-conditioning to equalize the cabin pressure to match that on the outside.

5. Your most pressing concern is to slow the aircraft down. Extend the wing flaps fully and as you approach the water your speed is crucial—too fast and you will break up on impact; too slow and the plane will "stall," the wings will lose their lift, and the plane will simply drop out of the air and break apart.

6. As you bring the plane into land, lift the nose up to twelve degrees, which is higher than a normal runway landing, and lower the tail end. You must land the plane absolutely level, otherwise the plane can break apart on impact, or one wing will clip the water sending the plane into a cartwheel. Try to skim the surface of the water like a pebble.

7. Once you have landed, close all air vents and openings to keep the aircraft buoyant in the water. The plane is designed to float long enough to evacuate your passengers.

8. Look on the bright side—things could have been a lot worse: you could have landed at LAX.

# 25. Eat Blowfish in Japan:

As culinary games of Russian roulette go, you can't live more dangerously than eating *fugu*—Japanese blowfish—a delicacy so poisonous that when prepared wrongly, the smallest amount of its venom can kill an adult human in less than thirty minutes (the ovaries, muscles, and liver contain a deadly poison). Here are a few tips to reduce the risk that you'll end the evening in respiratory and cardiac failure. However, your heart will miss a few beats when you see the bill: at the best restaurants one one serving of fugu can cost up to $250 per person.

## Sleeping with the Fishes

In Japan, about 10,000 tons of blowfish are consumed each year, but fatalities are actually on the decline as the strict laws and licences which govern preparation of the dish have been tightened.

Call up the restaurant in advance and warn them that you will be ordering fugu. Preparation is such an art that the restaurant may have to bring in a specialized sushi chef, so give them plenty of notice. Unless you are a valued and regular customer, any restaurant that is prepared to serve you fugu without a reservation should be avoided.

Fugu sashimi is very filling, and although it is very expensive, the portion size is usually enough to satisfy two diners. Eat at the sushi bar rather than the table so that you can see it being prepared; these moments may be your last on earth, so savor them.

## Delicate Taste

The fugu will be served in small thin strips with a radish dip accompaniment and a lime wedge. Only squirt on a few drops of lime (*sudachi*), and don't ruin the delicate taste with heaps of soy sauce (not only will you destroy the flavor, you'll appear uncouth). Eat slowly and wait for your lips and tongue to start tingling. This is normal, and not a sign that you are about to die; although if you lose feeling in your mouth or tongue, it's time to call an ambulance. You'll be dead by the time it arrives, but why not.

## Other Fish to Fry

There are about a hundred kinds of fugu worldwide, but the most poisonous, expensive, and delicious variety is *Tora-fugu*, and the best season to eat it is during the winter (when you will pay a premium).

n°: 23458403
26 NOV. 1998
Jamaïca

# 26. Buy on the Black Market:

Wherever there's a screwed up economy and a dysfunctional domestic policy, you'll find a thriving black market to match. It offers several services: currency exchange, goods cheaper than those in the legitimate market (often because you don't have to pay taxes); goods that are in short supply; cheap replicas or copies; and illegal items such as sexual services and equipment, drugs, weapons, and explosives.

## Currency

Beware of changing money on the streets or with private individuals. Don't flash your wad unless you want to get robbed. When your home currency is strong, carry mainly that; when your home currency is weak, carry the currency of the host country or a strong currency like Swiss francs. If your home currency is unstable, carry both. The safest way to use the black market is to haggle in the local market in the local currency and then at the last minute offer a lower figure in your home currency. High class joints generally won't get involved in this, and if you are just a short-stay tourist the risks of black-marketeering outweigh the benefits.

## Copyrighted Media

In many Asian countries you can buy ludicrously cheap copies of movies and music CDs, computer software and video games, as well as consumer electronics such as cell phones and gaming consoles. Buy "region-free" DVDs that can be played back home without special equipment. Never spend more than you can afford to lose. The items should be so cheap that you don't mind taking the risk on them either not working or not being what you think you're buying. There's no warranty or after sales support, and you may have to spend time reconfiguring the software when you get home (such as the 3G settings on your cell) and some will be only Asian and no use to you.

## Gas

In European countries where gas prices are high, if you rent a diesel car then you may be able to buy agricultural diesel (known as red diesel) cheaply from a corrupt and/or penniless farmer, or simply steal it between the hours of two and three in the morning. Don't put the stuff into your own car as it will ruin the engine.

## Replica Watches

Never buy an expensive replica; it's just not worth the money and you should be able to find something similar elsewhere for much less. Replicas differ enormously in quality. At the higher end, the exteriors are almost impossible to distinguish from the genuine product, even down to the manufacturer's logo and serial numbers. However, the insides will be cheap and generic, and will only last anywhere between a few months to a few years.

## Designer Clothes

The production of fake designer clothing and sneakers in developing countries is bigger than the manufacture of the genuine articles of some large brands such as Nike, Polo, and Levi's. Quality of fakes differs wildly. Large corporations never tire of warning us that fakes are always inferior to the genuine products, but this isn't always the case: some manufacturers of fakes take pride in making their products better than the overpriced originals. Check out the quality of fabric and the stitching, which should be tight, straight, and regular.

## Weapons

The best way to buy illegal weapons is to take a mini-vacation in Iraq, where you will be able to pick up brand new Glock 9-millimeter pistols, and immaculate, unused Kalashnikovs from post-Soviet Eastern European countries in the local open-air grocery stands. Thousands of US weapons intended to arm the Iraqi Army and police have found their way into the black market as well; plus, lots of weapons left in unguarded abandoned Iraqi military bases will be up for sale. Prices are rising as sectarian mistrust escalates out of control, so snap up a bargain now before the country descends into civil war after the coalition troops have pulled out.

# 27. Break More Ridiculous Laws Abroad:

If the following edicts represent the eye of the law then the law is an ass that needs a good slapping because it has lost the plot so completely it doesn't know whether to come or go.

1. In China, women aren't allowed to walk around naked in the privacy of their hotel room. They can only be naked in the bathroom.

2. In Denmark, it is illegal to start a car without first checking that there are no children sleeping underneath it, and an inn cannot charge you for food unless you consider yourself to be "full."

3. All electronic games are prohibited in Greece, including those on home computers, portable consoles, and cell phones. Even bringing a cell phone with game software into the country is illegal.

4. In Hong Kong, a woman may legally kill her cheating husband if she uses her bare hands. The woman with whom the husband is cheating can be killed in any manner.

5. In Italy, a woman of "ill repute or evil looks" entering a cheese factory in the area of Ferrara is breaking the law. A man may be arrested for wearing a skirt.

6. There are more than 100 offences that carry the death penalty in Iran. According to Article 49 of the Islamic Penal Code, the age of legal responsibility is nine for girls and fifteen for boys. A child's punishment for being raped is death. Iran is the only country that executes minors.

7. It is illegal to wear purple in Japan unless you are in mourning, and children aren't allowed to receive organ transplants. All foreign visitors must be photographed and fingerprinted.

8. Men in the Lebanon are legally permitted to have sex with animals, but only if the animals are female. It is illegal to have sex with a male animal (the punishment is death). Remember: straight bestiality good, gay bestiality bad.

9. In Russia, it is illegal to drive a dirty car, or be unemployed.

10. Saudi Arabian women aren't allowed to drive, or appear in public unless accompanied by a male relative or guardian, but a woman can divorce her husband if he doesn't supply her with enough coffee.

# 28. Venture into Mayan Ruins:

If you ever read *The Ruins* or saw the movie adaptation, you know that these ancient structures are extremely dangerous places for adventurous Americans to explore. Besides the fact that most of these ruins are archeological sites with very limited access, the ramifications for daring to enter such ancient grounds could be deadly. Seeing as how the collapse of the Maya culture is still heavily debated—there's a chance that the temples and other ruins are haunted. Angry spirits and deadly monsters are just as legitimate of a reason for the civilization's abrupt disappearance as an ecological disaster or foreign invasion, right?

## Where to Go

The Maya civilization extended from present-day southern Mexico down to El Salvador and Honduras. Your best bet if you dare to go wandering around the ancient cities is to head off to Belize. Fly into the capital city of Belmopan and then head towards the Guatemalan border. Pay a local to lead you through the Peten rainforest and off the beaten path from the Tikal National Park to some lesser-visited ruins of Caracol. You want to find some ancient remnants that aren't roped off and under constant watch.

## What You'll Find

Assuming you survived the rainforest trek and that your local guide did not rob you and leave you stranded, you will now be able to wander through the remnants of one of the largest Maya kingdoms. Caracol contains all the staples of Maya civilization and you should be able to locate a number of the society's typical constructions.

Try to find an observatory. Most tour guides who lead groups through the ruins call out round temples as being observatories. Therefore, if you see a round building, it's an observatory. The Mayas built observatories in order to validate their theories about time as well as celestial bodies and events. In fact, the Maya calendar, based on astronomical observations, is the basis for many apocalyptic 2012 myths. See if you can gain any insight to the end of the world by entering one of these ancient structures. If you do, you can hit up the talk show circuit and make a ton of money. Just be sure to spend it all before 2013.

# 29. Find Atlantis:

In 370 B.C., the Greek philosopher Plato wrote about the lost city of Atlantis in two books, *Timaeus* and *Critias*. He didn't invent the idea though, he drew upon the writings of the Greek ruler Solon, which preceded him by two hundred years. Plato reckoned that the once prosperous island of Atlantis had disappeared under the sea ten thousand years earlier. Before its destruction, he says that it had been a powerful state that ruled parts of Europe and Africa, but the greed of the inhabitants angered the god Zeus, who punished them with violent earthquakes and floods. Scholars have argued that Plato got the dates wrong by mistranslating Solon, and that Atlantis was in fact the Minoan island of Santorini, destroyed by a volcanic eruption in 1470 B.C.

## Bimini Road

One of the more implausible Atlantean theories centers on the Bimini Road in the Bahamas, where sunken stone formations were interpreted in the early twentieth century by the psychic Edgar Cayce as being a sunken harbor. Cayce and his followers believed they were re-incarnated Atlanteans, so that further explains his argument against the fact that these formations are naturally occurring beach rock, which have been carbon-dated to between 2,000 and 4,000 years old. As absurd reasons for visiting beautiful places go, you can't get a better one than this.

## Cuba

In 2001, a Canadian team of oceanographers placed Atlantis off the coast of Cuba. They discovered strange geometrical formations of rocks spread over eight square miles, and nearly half a mile deep, along with an extinct volcano and fault lines. They prevail that the complex was above sea level until an earthquake 8,000 years ago made it vanish.

## Take Your Pick

Other possible locations are off the coast of Cyprus in the Mediterranean Sea, near Indonesia, near Puerto Rico (before it was destroyed by a six-mile-wide asteroid), Sardinia, Finland, the Black Sea, and Turkey.

So basically, pick your vacation destination and you'll be bound to find a local site that claims to be the true Atlantis. Fortunately for you, *Man From Atlantis*, the short-lived science fiction television series that ran for just thirteen episodes and four movies is much easier to track down. You can pick up complete VHS-to-DVD copies on dodgy internet sites for less than $30, or P2P torrents for free.

# 30. Have a Sinful Weekend in Sin City:

You don't have to be a superstar or billionaire to make Vegas your playground. Sin City makes most of its money from the little people like you, especially at the casinos.

## Hit the Casinos

We've all heard the joke that it's easy to walk away from a casino with a small fortune—arrive with a large one. When you're playing the tables most casinos have a minimum bet level of $5 or $10, but lots of smaller places like Bill's Saloon or Casino Royale have lower minimums. Slots A Fun has tables with a $1 minimum most nights of the week. Remember, to stay sober (don't accept all the free drinks), don't bet more than you can afford to lose, don't press your bets, and quit while you're ahead, so you've got enough of your bankroll left to hire a hooker and/or get married.

## Pick Up a Hooker

It's not legal in Vegas, but there are hookers everywhere, and it's sort of tolerated. If you hang around alone in one of the hotel bars looking well dressed and rich, you'll probably get hit on by an escort. If so, be clear up front about what she's offering, otherwise you could be paying for her to hang off your arm all evening and nothing more. The best way to guarantee some action is to phone the numbers in newspaper ads from the Strip and downtown, or you may get handed a flyer in the street. The services are usually called something like "bachelor guide" and have a good choice of ladies, but don't expect her to look like her photo. Now at least, they'll be no misunderstanding of what you both want. Be careful though, you can't go to the cops if it all goes wrong.

## The King of Nuptials

Romantically, if your mantra is "I know, let's go get married, just for the hell of it!" then Las Vegas is the place to do it. You'll be following in the footsteps of some of the greats: Elvis Presley, Britney Spears, and Angelina Jolie all tied the knot in Vegas. Why shouldn't you become one half of the nearly 120,000 couples who get married there every year? Sin City is the only place in the world where you can get married by "Elvis," and with the King officiating at your nuptials you will have some world-class memories no one can take away—even if you sober up and apply for an annulment within seventy-two hours. You should get about ten minutes pre-ceremony to hammer out the particulars. Don't forget to buy your official marriage license application at the Clark County

Courthouse the day before the big one. Hours are 8 A.M. to midnight, seven days a week, and the cost is $55. (Valentine's Day and New Year's Eve are peak times to avoid.) Bring ID and proof of age if you are under 21, plus your Social Security Number. You'll also need written consent from your parents or guardians if either of you is under 18.

If you're getting hitched on the cheap, remember that hotel prices are lowest when the midsummer temperatures are highest. You will sweat buckets during the ceremony, but at least you'll have more money in your pocket to play the slots.

# 31. Survive a Plane Crash:

There is plenty you can do to improve your chances of surviving a plane crash. In the US alone, between 1983 and 2000, there were 568 plane crashes, of which more than 95 percent of passengers survived. Smoke inhalation and fire accounts for more than a third of fatalities.

## Avoid Manmade Fibers

Travel in cotton and natural fibers. Manmade fibers will melt onto your skin in a fire. Also, keep your shoes on during landing.

## Have an Escape Plan

Pay attention to the safety instructions at the start of the flight. Take a look around and you'll be amazed how many people aren't listening; their inattention reduces their chances of survival (and yours if they get in your way). Count how many rows of seats there are between you and the nearest exit so that you can find your way in the dark (or in smoke) by touch alone. You may have to trample over the heads of some of these arrogant losers to reach safety.

## Get the Safest Seat

Some say the safest seats are over the wing, which are near the exit row, located in the strongest part of the plane. However, if there's an engine fire, it's one of the worst places to sit. Statistically, the safest seats are in the rear, where survival rates are 69 percent as opposed to 56 percent over the wing and 49 percent at the front of the plane. In individual cases, the safest seats depend on how the plane crashes, but knowing where your nearest exit, and/or being close to an exit are your top priorities.

## Survive the Impact

Pull the seat belt as tight as possible. There's a good reason for adopting the brace position—placing your head over your knees and holding onto your calves, and getting your upper body as low down as possible—it reduces whiplash and stops you from flying forward and hitting the seat in front of you. (The brace position also protects your teeth so that your corpse can be identified using dental records.) When booking your flight, bear in mind that the brace position is often impossible in an economy seat. Place your feet flat on the floor, farther back than your knees, and wedge something soft under the seat in front to act as a cushion (lots of people break their legs below the knee on impact).

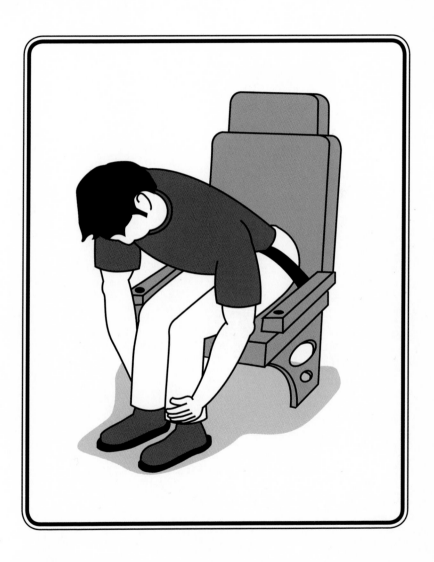

## Release the Seatbelt

Flick away; don't press. Many people waste precious time trying to unlock their seatbelt the wrong way. They are used to the push-button release used in cars, and under pressure they revert to this pressing action, when they should be unclasping the buckle by flicking the latch away from them.

## Don't Inhale Smoke

Hold your breath or wrap a wet handkerchief around your mouth and nose to filter out some of the smoke (better still, pack a smoke hood in your carry-on). Just a few breaths of toxic smoke can render you unconscious. If you get your eyes and nose at floor level, you will avoid the smoke, but risk getting trampled by other passengers. Keep in mind cabin, floor lights are red, but turn green at the exits.

## Listen for Instructions but Don't Wait for Them

Pay attention to instructions from the flight attendants, but if none are forthcoming, don't sit there doing nothing. Those around you may be in shock and will just sit as if stuck in their seats, while others panic and block the exits within seconds. Don't wait. Get moving and calmly head for the nearest exit. Get yourself out. Don't stop to help family and friends or you'll all die.

# 32. Survive in the Australian Outback:

*G'day mate!* There's a harsh reality to the friendly Australian people's backyard. The Outback is not a single place, but instead is the general term used by Aussies to refer to any part of the country that is not densely populated—which is virtually the whole thing. That means there's a lot of land to cover, tons of nature to see, and all sorts of trouble to find yourself in.

Get a start on your Outback adventure by renting a 4x4 in a northern city like Darwin and head south. The smart move would be to stick to the mapped highways and avoid going off-road. However, chances are you are not interested in smart moves. You will most likely find yourself completely lost. And that is when your real troubles will begin.

## Outback Jackass

Besides the wide variety of snakes and spiders that are likely to deliver a poisonous bite when you go wandering outside your vehicle, the incredible heat of the Outback is a very big threat. There's a real danger to walking long distances while the sun is fully out as a bout of heatstroke will leave you incapacitated and easy pickings for a pack of wild dingoes. Unless you are left with no other option, stay in your 4x4 and sightsee from the driver's seat.

## Crocodile Dundee-in-Training

Do NOT go near any bodies of water. No matter how hot you are and how tempting a dip in the river may seem, jumping in is an invitation to a feast where you are the main course. The Australian saltwater crocodile patrols the waters of northern Australia, with a typical male coming in at about fifteen feet long and weighing around 2,000 lbs. Just because you are away from the coastline does not mean you are safe from this territorial predator. The Australian saltwater crocodile is known to journey inland down freshwater rivers.

If you do happen to find yourself nose-to-snout with one of these beasts, you can try to defend yourself by holding the animal's snout closed. The animal's jaw has an extremely strong biting power, but a significantly weaker ability to open. Clamp the jaw down and hold on for a ride—it will likely be a short one.

## Captain Those Kangaroos

A staple of the Australian Outback, the kangaroo is a dangerous adversary when it comes to road travel. The animal has been known to jump in front of cars when startled. And with a leaping speed of about 30 MPH, it can cause quite the collision. Be careful as you travel down the roads and be mindful of the many kangaroo crossing signs you will see.

# 33. Break Absurd U.S. Laws:

The United States can hold its head high when it comes to showing the rest of the world how to pass dumb state laws. Passing them must have seemed like a good idea at the time.

1. In Alabama, you can be arrested for operating a vehicle blindfolded, wearing a fake moustache that causes laughter in church, flicking boogers in the wind, and keeping an ice cream cone in your back pocket.

2. In California, it is against the law for anyone to stop a child from jumping over puddles of water, and a city ordinance states anyone who detonates a nuclear device within city limits as well will be fined $500.

3. Illinois law expressly forbids giving lighted cigars to dogs, cats, and other domesticated pets. Eating in a restaurant that is on fire, peeing in your neighbor's mouth, and drinking beer out of a bucket while sitting on the curb are all off limits.

4. In Louisiana, biting someone with your natural teeth is simple assault, but if you have false teeth you will be charged with aggravated assault. Having a pizza delivered to someone without their permission will land you with a $500 fine.

5. Minnesota law prohibits walking across the Minnesota-Wisconsin border with a duck on your head; giving or receiving oral sex; and having sex with your wife if your breath stinks of garlic, onions, or sardines.

6. When committing a murder in New Jersey, it is illegal to wear a bullet-proof vest. You're not allowed to pump your own gas, and in Newark it is illegal to buy ice cream after 6:00 P.M.

7. You can get arrested in Ohio for getting a fish drunk, or sharing a house with more than four other women (if you're a woman). In Oxford, it's illegal for a woman to strip off her clothing while standing in front of a man's picture.

8. In South Dakota, lying down and falling asleep in a cheese factory is actionable behavior, and movies that show cops being beaten up are banned.

9. In Utah, you are breaking the law if you persistently tread on the cracks between paving stones on the sidewalk of a state highway. Also, you cannot have sex in the back of an ambulance while it is responding to an emergency call.

10. Three ways to get arrested in Wyoming are being drunk in a mine, wearing a hat in a theater that obstructs other people's views, and taking a picture of a rabbit from January to April without an official permit.

# 34. Traffic in Cultural Antiquities:

The growth of tourism, the internationalization of the art market, and the 2003 invasion of Iraq mean that there has rarely been a better time for you to get involved in the trafficking of cultural antiquities.

## Elgin Marbles

The benchmark by which all looters should measure themselves is of course, Thomas Bruce, 7th Earl of Elgin, who, in the early nineteenth century, removed the famous Elgin Marbles from the Parthenon in Greece, and hauled them back to Britain along with a piece of paper from the Ottoman Empire saying that he had won them fair and square in a game of Kerplunk. After a brief debate, Parliament decided that Elgin was a bloody good bloke and should be patted on the back for bagging such spiffy souvenirs. The British Museum bought them off him and they are now on display in the specially-built Duveen gallery (once a custom-made wing has been built to house your looted treasures, you know that they are staying put).

## Provenance

As men with dark robes and gavels like to say, when it comes to stealing stuff from other countries, success depends upon provenance, provenance, *provenance*. If you don't have a paper trail proving that you acquired the artifacts legitimately, you may as well keep them under your bed at home because you won't be able to sell them on the international art market. Only kidding: there has always been a flourishing trade in stolen treasures, and just about every museum and auction house in the world is complicit.

## The Price of Democracy

Be prepared to travel to places that other people are flee-ing, namely war zones. Even though the wholesale looting of Iraq's museums and archaeological sites has been going on for five years, there is still plenty of stuff being dug out of the ground daily (some estimates are as high as 15,000 artifacts every day), and still no one is stopping it. However, you will have to fend off all the Iraqis who are plundering their own national heritage in the name of *zakat*, the Islamic principle that everything belongs to God and wealth is held by humans in trust. This makes it OK for them to sell looted goods to fund insurgency against coalition forces. In the words of the great political philosopher Donald Rumsfeld, "Democracy is messy."

n°: 23456405 VISA

26 NOV. 1998

Jamaïca

# 35. Have Sex on a Beach:

Making love on a beach is many people's fantasy, and as fantasies go, it is quite achievable. Just get yourself down to the nearest coastline with your partner and make like rabbits. The chance of getting caught, plus the sound of the waves lapping at your feet, with a huge red sun sinking below the horizon, is an appealing scenario. The reality will probably be otherwise—and is it really any different to screwing in the park or behind a dumpster? It's all in the mind. If you get intimate at the seaside, be prepared for three things to happen, (besides getting arrested):

1. You will be secretly filmed by someone hiding in the dunes, and your coupling will be available somewhere on the Internet by the end of the week. That is a certainty. Know that it will happen and live with the consequences. Choose your location carefully. And if you think making love in the water will be better, you'll get filmed by more than one person. Even if you think there's no way you

could be spotted, you'll be wrong. Your actions will end up on a mainframe somewhere, even if it's the database of a Russian satellite, or the live feed from a coastguard helicopter. Take a blanket to provide some cover.

2. Beaches are covered in sand. Now, you may be dimly aware of this fact on a superficial level, so let's spell it out again: S-A-N-D. Among the many properties enjoyed by granulated rock, the fact that it gets everywhere and there's nothing you can do about it, no matter how many towels you bring, is most important. This means that a certain amount of frictional discomfort is inevitable and you will spend days chasing sand out of the most intimate places.

3. The sex will not live up to your expectations, in the same way that the lesbian kiss in *Vicky Cristina Barcelona*, making love in front of an open fridge, and trying to recreate the butter scene from *Last Tango in Paris* were ultimately disappointments. It will be neither as good nor as bad as most people want to tell you it is! Keep your hopes low and you may be pleasantly surprised.

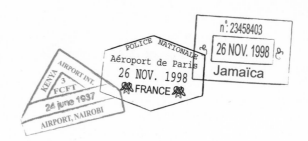

# 36. Upgrade Your Hotel Room:

Upgrading your room isn't always possible—but if you don't ask, you don't get. If you follow these instructions, you can improve your chances of getting more than you paid for.

1. The most important factor is probably loyalty. If you travel a lot, try to stay in the same hotel whenever possible, and always be nice to the staff. Make a point of getting to know the general manager so that he or she recognizes your face the next time you ask for an upgrade. In some hotels, you can also trade frequent flier miles for upgrades. When you make the reservation, always ask what is available, including special deals. After your stay, tip well, and send the manager a hand-written letter of thanks. Praise for good service is always remembered.

2. Try to bring business to the hotel. Book corporate events there, or recommend the hotel to friends and make sure they mention your name when they check in. This all helps to build a micro-network of mutual benefit. If you make the hotel extra money, they will be only too happy to

show their gratitude by giving you an upgrade, which costs them nothing, but makes a big difference to you.

3. Even if you don't travel frequently, dress like a seasoned business traveler; the hotel will try harder to accommodate you than if you look like a dumb tourist. Similarly, if you have booked into the lowest budget room in the hotel, you will look like a cheapskate. Booking the second cheapest room gives you more leverage.

4. If you are visiting a hotel for the first time—and aren't concerned with building a future relationship— complain about any aspect of the experience with which you are unsatisfied, and make it clear that you are prepared to be placated with some freebies. For example, if your room is dirty or in a noisy hallway, it is reasonable to insist on a room change (plus an upgrade for the inconvenience caused).

5. Before you ask for an upgrade, decide exactly what it is you want to get out of it. If a larger bed or a swankier bathroom is more important than a larger room, make this clear. Maybe you are looking for absolute quiet, or you are prepared to compromise on a room above the bar, so long as they can offer you something extra.

6. Generally the higher floors have the best rooms, so use some charm and claim you are new to their wonderful city and would appreciate a great view of it from your room. Who can refuse you when you put it like that?

7. Check in as late as possible, as the staff will have a clearer idea what's available.

8. Offer to pay a little bit extra. This shows that you are interested in comfort rather than getting something for nothing. The chances are that they'll give you an upgrade and brush away your kind offer.

# 37. Prevent International Faux Pas:

When you travel abroad, remember that you are the foreigner, and should try to avoid stepping on any cultural toes. For example, just because you've been wiping your backside for years doesn't mean you're doing it right.

1. In Arab countries, eat food, shake hands, and generally interact with the world using your right hand, as they wipe their backside using their left. When you're in one of these countries, don't even use your left hand for pointing or beckoning. Also, if your private stash of toilet paper runs out, don't resort to newspaper because if the name Allah appears anywhere on the page, and you wipe your backside with it . . . well, you can see the problem.

2. In Greece and Bulgaria, nodding the head upwards means "no" and tilting the head from side to side means "yes." Even more confusing, the Greek word for yes is *nai*.

3. In most parts of Europe and the United States, maintaining good eye contact is usually a sign of attentiveness and trustworthiness. However, this isn't the case in many Asian and African countries, where averting the eyes is a sign of respect and/or deference, and prolonged eye contact is perceived as a threat. The same applies in Mexico.

4. Kissing in public (even a peck) can land you in lots of trouble in many Arab and Asian countries, and may even get you arrested. Watch who you kiss too. Remember the uproar Richard Gere caused when he kissed across Shilpa Shetty in India? Or when Mickey Rooney "respectfully" kissed the hand of Queen Elizabeth II in Washington D.C.?

5. When in Thailand, never pat anyone on the head (even a child). This is very rude, since the head is the highest part of the body symbolically (and literally) and is held in the highest regard. Likewise, it is rude to show or point the soles of your feet—the lowest point of the body—towards others.

6. In many Asian countries, including Japan, when someone hands you their business card it is very rude to just stuff it unread into your pocket. Treat the card with great reverence. Hold it with both hands, read it attentively, and don't write on it.

7. Don't tip people in China. It's illegal and will cause much embarrassment.

8. Gift giving is popular in many cultures, but never offer leather goods to an Indian or a Hindu anywhere in the world. In Singapore and Japan, don't single out individuals—make it clear that your gift is to everyone. Conversely in Arab countries, don't make a big show of admiring the possessions of others, as they may feel obliged to give them to you.

9. In Muslim countries, if anyone sees you eating or drinking during the hours of daylight (strictly, from the first call to prayer until sunset) during the month of Ramadam, you will not only cause great offense, you will probably get arrested, and ignorance is not an excuse. Sexual thoughts and activities are also prohibited during daylight hours.

10. When in Austria, beware of drafts—the Austrians are terrified of them—so they avoid having two windows opposite each other open, and on public transportation, you will find that the windows on one side of the vehicle are kept locked.

Aéroport de Paris
26 NOV. 1998
FRANCE

VISA

# 38. Start a Motorcycle Gang:

Starting a bike gang isn't as easy as it used to be. A few decades ago, it was simply a matter of riding your hog down a dark alley and gathering together a collection of social misfits, sociopaths, and criminals. Today bike-riding crazies are a dying breed (or lifers) and harder to find than a horny panda, so you have to be more inventive to track them down.

## Start a Fight

Walk into the roughest bar in town, and challenge the assembled company to a fight with the weapon of choice for the aspiring motorcycle gang member: the pool cue. Anyone who accepts your challenge can join, but not until you've spent half-an-hour trading blows and trashing the joint. This form of recruitment appears frequently in the movies—big hairy men beat the crap out of each other to earn mutual respect.

## Squares Need Not Apply

If you live in a more upmarket neighborhood, instead of fighting, hand out application forms. Anyone who carries a pen on their person, or who actually fills in the form, is clearly unsuitable, whereas those who make a nihilistic gesture of rejection, such as setting your questionnaire on fire, or pulling down their pants and pissing on it, pass with honors.

Tattoos, beards, broken noses, scars, or a T-shirt slogan alluding to the ontological duality within biking culture (e.g. "Ride or die") are also highly desirable.

## Naming Your Gang

Think of a name for your gang that implies menace but is also basic enough so that the illiterate members can paint it on their jackets. Also, everyone should adopt a road name. Decide whether you want your gang to be a weekend activity or a way of life on the wrong side of the law. If biking and brotherhood is your life calling, then technically you are what is known in biking circles as a One Percenter, and should wear a One Percenter patch (this is a diamond or rhombus shape). If even this is too conformist for you, then why not cut off your arms and live in a barrel. Seriously, when are you going to meet the world half way?

## Stay Safe

In today's health-conscious society, it is reasonable to allow non-smokers to join, but don't compromise with road safety: make sure everyone knows their turn signals. There's a time and a place for pulling wheelies and burning out your back tire, but flagrant disregard of the Highway Code takes the rebel ethos a step too far.

# 39. Travel Across America for Free:

In 2007, three friends decided to fund their road trip across the US by selling ad space on every inch of their van, as well as their own clothes. Did you hear about them? Where are they now?

## Cash Road Trip

They set up the website *www. cashroadtripusa.com* (now defunct) and they charged about $100 per square foot on their van, and up to $7,500 per day for wearing a company's T-shirt. They aimed to become driving and walking billboard posters and keep a video blog of their trip to attract lots of media coverage en route and give the advertizers added value.

## Million Pixels

It sounds like an idea that can't fail, especially since it follows the same principle that worked so well in 2005 when Alex Tew, a twenty-one-year-old from Wiltshire, England founded *www.milliondollarhomepage.com.* His simple aim was to make a million dollars by selling 1,000,000 pixels for $1 each. The site went live on August 26, 2005, and, it made a gross total of

$1,037,100 in five months, so Alex deferred college in order to count his cash.

## Your Journey

Bear in mind that you will actually have to make your road trip; you can't just take the money and stay in your bedroom. Also, you might not make a dime. If you do a search for the three friends's website, you'll get an error message, and there's not much follow-up information about them either, so it's hard to judge how successful they were. Still, that shouldn't stop you from trying it out. It isn't a foregone conclusion that the country will think you're a freeloading scrounger and ignore you.

## Foot the Bill

-VISA-

Your fallback position is simple: walk. It's the best way to see a country; it's free (except for the sponsorship you'll raise to pay for your van-driving support team); it's good exercise; and it will expose you to all sorts of character-building and life-enhancing experiences that you wouldn't get by sitting on a Greyhound bus listening to your iPod. In the late '80s Ffyona Campbell, an eighteen-year-old British long-distance walker, crossed the United States on foot from New York to Los Angeles, but her sponsorship commitments and personal problems turned the trip into a nightmare for her. So maybe your best option is to avoid the pressures of sponsorship and just head off with a backpack and don't tell anyone where you're going; beg, steal, and trash-forage for food along the way. When Peter Jenkins walked across America in the '70s he said, "I started out searching for myself and my country, and found both." You can't get a better endorsement than that.

# 40. Sail Through the Bermuda Triangle:

The Bermuda Triangle (a.k.a. the Devil's Triangle, Hell's Armpit, Beelzebub's Shower Stall, Mrs. Satan's Ladygarden, etc.) is a region in the northwestern Atlantic Ocean covering an area of 500,000 square miles where literally hundreds of ships, planes, and ocean liners have vanished during the last century.

## Plotting the Triangle

The three points of the Triangle are Miami, Bermuda, and San Juan, Puerto Rico. Although, some people include the Azores, the Gulf of Mexico, and the West Indies in the Triangle, making it more of a trapezoid shape. It is without doubt the most dangerous place to sail, fly, or float on a raft without food or water on the planet bar none.

## Safe Passage

So how can you sail through the Triangle and come out the other side? Well, that depends

on what you believe is the cause of all the mysterious disap-
pearances. Sudden storms can flare up without warning in any
part of the ocean, especially during the hurricane season, so
try to avoid making the journey during summer to late fall.

## Crews Control

The Gulf Stream flows through the Triangle traveling at
about six knots, so if your engine breaks down (if you haven't
got an engine, forget it), and someone on board smashes your
communications equipment with a baseball bat, then you could
quickly find yourself adrift and lost. Just don't hire any
borderline psychotics when choosing your crew.

POLICE NATIONALE
Aéroport de Paris
26 NOV. 1998
🞕 FRANCE 🞕

## Look Up to the Sky

The Triangle is also said to be an area where the needle of a compass becomes unreliable and sends you way off course. If this happens, ignore your compass and navigate by the stars, or use your GPS, which shouldn't be affected by magnetic anomalies.

## Three Tweets to the Wind

Another theory to explain boats sinking without a trace is the release of large quantities of methane hydrates from the continental shelves. These gases turn the water into a bubbling maelstrom in which ships lose their buoyancy and get sucked under the waves. Guard against this natural hazard by bringing a canary, which should die when it breathes methane, or carbon monoxide, or something like that.

## Storm in a Tea Cup

Actually, most of these precautions should be unnecessary anyway because, statistically, the number of ships and planes that have disappeared is no higher than elsewhere, and many of the reported losses were of ships outside the Triangle, or ones that turned up later. So basically, don't worry about it. You'll be OK—probably.

# 41. Travel to the Past:

Physicists tell us that backwards time travel is very unlikely since it potentially throws up an infinite number of possible problems of causality (often summed up by the idea of killing your grandfather in the past so that you cease to exist in the present because you were never born). However, the Novikov self-consistency principle (the idea that only self-consistent trips back in time would be permitted) and the parallel universes theory both deal with the problem of causality. With that sorted, here are some topical ways to travel into the past.

## Make a Wormhole

Professor Stephen Hawking has theorized that "if you can travel from one side of the galaxy, to the other, in a week or two, you could go back through another wormhole, and arrive back before you set out." When the giant Hadron Collider in Cern, Switzerland was switched on in September 2008, two Russian mathematicians predicted that it might create the right conditions for the production of tiny wormholes through time-space. Then it broke down. It cost more then $10 billion, and it requires a lot of space, so it's not really practical for backyard time travel on a budget. Also, the wormholes would be so small that you wouldn't be able to fit through.

## Spielberg Method

This well-known fictional method involves using a nuclear-powered DeLorean as a time machine. Set the date you want to travel to, then drive the car until it reaches 88 miles per hour, at which point the nuclear reaction will generate the 1.21 gigawatts of power required for time travel. The flaw with this design is that refined plutonium is not available any further back in time than the mid twentieth-century, rendering the nuclear reactor defunct. The only comparable source of power is in lightning.

## Hiro Nakamura Method

This requires intense concentration. Close your eyes and furrow your brow, and concentrate really hard on stopping time. Your control will improve over time, and if you can locate the sword of Takezo Kensei you should be able to focus your powers and teleport yourself and a friend through space and time relatively easily.

## Christopher Reeve Method

All serious discussions of time travel should include *Somewhere in Time*, the best movie on the subject ever made. It's a great love story and it posits a kind of astral projection that is the best domestic method of time travel to explore.

At the beginning of the movie, an old lady approaches Christopher Reeve, presses a pocket watch into his hand, and pleads, "Come back to me." She goes back to her hotel and dies that night in May 1972. Eight years later, he stays at the same old hotel and falls in love with the picture of a woman (Jane Seymour) in a photo taken in 1912 that is on display. He resolves to travel back in time to have sex with her. He buys clothes from the period, cuts his hair in the style of the time, clears everything modern out of his hotel room, and then records a monologue on a cassette tape designed to hypnotize him into thinking with absolute certainty that he is lying on his bed in 1912. After realizing that the modern tape recorder is hampering his attempt, he tucks it under his bed, and finally succeeds in willing himself back in time. After all the sex, he pulls a modern coin out of his pocket, which jolts him back to 1980. She is left holding his pocket watch and screaming his name. He tries to go back in time again but the spell is broken. He pines away and dies in his present time, and the lovers are reunited in the clouds. The moral of the story is that when a man wants sex badly enough, even time travel is possible.

# 42. Get Felt Up by a Japanese Chikan:

n°: 23458403

20 NOV 1998

Jamaïca

VISA

*Chikan* (痴漢, チカン, or ちかん) is a Japanese term which means "pervert," but has predominantly come to mean "train groper." It describes people who rub up against others and cop a feel on crowded public transportation. Japanese cities are a chikan paradise because many of the trains and buses are packed to bursting, so there is plenty of opportunity for them to indulge their seedy little urges.

## Suffering in Silence

Ask any woman in Japan whether she has been molested, and she'll likely say that she has. In fact, it's hard to find a woman who hasn't. Generally, the women don't cause a scene. They don't scream or yell, and they can't move away because the train is so packed. They keep respectfully quiet because they are too embarrassed to make a fuss. Also, people who are watching it won't intervene, although they may send the offender a scornful look. The authorities have tried to stop it by designating certain carriages as women only at peak times, but the problem is still of epidemic proportions. The unintended consequence is that women who ride in the other carriages are now seen as fair game. In Japan, more than 4,000 men are arrested each year for groping on public transportation.

## Pretty Vacant

So if you're in Tokyo but you haven't had any action for a while and you feel like some anonymous human contact, travel at peak time on the Odakyu line, which has some of the most crowded trains on the network. The Inogashira line is also notorious for chikans. Board the first or last carriages of a train. These are the main chikan hunting grounds because they can run away more easily (since the exits on the platform are at either end and there is less chance of getting caught up in the crowds). Chikans are also said to prey on women who are walking really slow, and who look dumb. So if you want to get felt up, lower your IQ by thirty points and try to look as timid and demure as possible.

If you feel any unusual or ambiguous contact, this is just the beginning. Chikans do a little test first, to see if you react. Keep quiet and they'll go further. By the time you reach your stop, you should be riding the rainbow to Shibuya.

POLICE NATIONALE
Aéroport de Paris
26 NOV. 1998
FRANCE

# 43. Cause a Ruckus in Singapore:

Singapore is often described as a "fine" country, because it is so easy to get fined there. Here are five ways to part with your cash and in some cases your liberty.

1. In 1992, it became illegal to chew or own gum in Singapore. Chewing gum is a cleaning nightmare in any country, but the impetus for the complete ban came after the $5 billion metro system (MRT) was opened in 1987. This was the largest public works program ever undertaken in the country and its success was a matter of national pride. However, when vandals started sticking chewing gum on the train door sensors, the Prime Minister Goh Chok Tong took decisive action and instituted a total ban. The importing of chewing gum was immediately stopped, and shops were given a grace period in which to sell their remaining stock. However, in 2004 this law was relaxed slightly to allow the sale and use of medicinal chewing gum. This concession was part of a US-Singapore Free Trade Agreement, which will save the Singapore economy about $150 million in duty.

2. If you fail to flush a public toilet after you have used it, you face a $150 fine. Also, if you get the urge to urinate in an elevator, be aware that some elevators are equipped with special detectors which jam the doors closed when they detect urine, and won't open again until the authorities arrive to fine you.

3. Dropping litter incurs a fine of up to $1,000 for a first offense and up to twice this amount for repeat offenders, plus community service cleaning duties. Littering the floor with the contents of your sinuses (i.e. spitting) is also a finable offense. Be a responsible citizen and take your loogies home with you.

4. There used to be a lot of fatal accidents involving people walking across bus parking areas, so in 2003, jaywalking anywhere became a punishable offense. You face an on-the-spot fine of up to $500 for the first time, up to double for second offenses, and up to six months in jail for repeat offenders.

5. There is a mandatory death penalty for anyone caught smuggling or dealing drugs, and long prison sentences for possession and using.

# 44. Protect Against a Tiger Attack:

If you are backpacking around India or Asia and you are running short on funds, you might want to consider skipping the expensive hotel or hostel and sleeping off the beaten path in the woods. However, opting to camp to save cash presents one big risk: tigers.

## Odds in Your Favor

Tigers are an endangered species; only about 5,000 to 7,500 tigers are left in the wild. You will likely luck out and a hungry tiger will not wake you from your sleep. Instead, a poisonous snake will probably bite you. Sweet dreams!

## Night Walker

If you do find yourself in tiger territory though, chances are you will be attacked in your sleep. Tigers are typically nocturnal hunters. With tigers coming in at about ten feet long and weighing approximately 400 to 570 lbs, you really don't stand a chance. Even if it isn't completely dark out, the tiger's stripes are perfect camouflage for the long grass you're probably settling down in.

The tiger will likely stalk your campsite in perfect silence before leaping out and pouncing on you. An adult tiger has an average horizontal leap of about fifteen feet. So you probably won't hear it pouncing until after it has its paws on your chest and is biting at your throat. At least it will be so quick you won't feel (most of) the pain.

## Protect Your Campsite

A smart choice if you do make the stupid one to camp in the Asian wilderness is to fortify your site. Here are some suggestions:

**Booby trap:** dig a few ditches around your site and cover them up with some small branches and leaves. When the tiger circles your camp sizing you up, chances are it will fall into one of the hidden holes. (If it works in the movies, it has to in real life, right?)

**Bird lime:** spread a sticky mixture of mustard oil and latex around your site so that the tiger will step in the goo. When it tries to clean itself, it will transfer the stickiness onto its face. Dust, leaves, and other debris will now stick to the tiger's face and hamper its vision, making it unable to hunt.

**Spikes:** sharpen some bamboo rods into spikes and then drive them into the ground around your site, with the pointy ends sticking out. If you have enough time and energy to sharpen and build this type of barricade before nightfall, you should be safe—from tigers; this sort of thing won't stop those poisonous snakes.

# 45. Pick Up a Flight Attendant :

Everyone secretly dreams about picking up a flight attendant. They are glamorous, wear sexy uniforms, and are a sexually ambiguous hybrid of servant and master—they have to indulge your every whim, but they are also in charge and would think nothing of restraining you if you were to become belligerent. They are also trained to sit on aggressive customers. Mmmm. Add artificial cabin pressure at 30,000 feet to the mix and you have an explosive libidinous cocktail. But how do you pick one up?

## Dream Ticket

Flight attendants may seem like bilingual flying goddesses, but they are human. They suffer the same frailties and insecurities as other women on minimum wage, and are looking for the same things in a potential partner: an airline pilot with a quarter-of-a-million dollar salary, a rock star, or a millionaire. If prompted they will also say that a great sense of humor is important, but don't be fooled. Here are five top pick-up tips:

1. Virgin and British Airways have the sexiest while Emirates and Singapore airlines host a bounty of Asian babes, but the most hittable-on attendants work for the budget airlines. They are undervalued and underpaid, and have the lowest job satisfaction and self-esteem, allegedly. They aren't as easy on the eyes, but they are up for a bit of rough trade with a well-dressed businessman traveling in First Class (see "Get Bumped Up to First Class" on page 16).

2. There's no point hitting on her after she has worked three shifts back to back. Sure, you want her to be tired and less guarded at the end of a flight, but not so exhausted that she just wants to sleep for twelve hours. So don't bother chatting up the attendants on a long haul flight; stick to domestic or short international flights.

3. If you are a frequent flyer, use the same airline, so there's more chance of seeing the same faces and building up a relationship. Some girls are after more than a quick romp and like to get to know you first.

4. Rent an airline pilot uniform from a costume shop. Not only will you be given preferential treatment on board, you are guaranteed to score plenty of duty-free tail in a nice foreign hotel.

5. If you happen to be a British movie star and want some in-flight action, fly Qantas every time.

# 46. Swim with Piranhas:

The jagged razor-sharp interlocking teeth of a piranha make it a fearsome predator (it can even bite through a steel fishing hook). Its name means "toothfish." A school of piranhas can strip a piece of meat to the bone in a matter of seconds, so if you have to cross piranha-infested waters it's best to take precautions to minimize the risk of being attacked.

Most species of piranha live in fresh water in South America, particularly in the Amazonian, Guianas, and Paraguayan river systems. They prefer still or slow moving streams or lakes and they cannot survive in cold water. They form large groups mainly for defense rather than to hunt.

## Feeding Pattern

Piranhas are omnivorous, and can be both scavengers and predators. They mainly eat fish, plants, and insects, but they will also feed on dead animals or attack live ones that have fallen into the water. When water levels are high your risk of being attacked is virtually nil, but during the dry season, when food is scarce, they will become desperate and take whatever they can get. During low water season they are themselves more vulnerable to attack from predators such as dolphins and caimans (a type of crocodilian reptile), so piranhas are more aggressive at these times.

Piranhas are day feeders and they rest at night, so that is the best time to avoid them. Although, you are at greater risk of being attacked by other night-feeding predators such as caimans. However, caimans tend to stop feeding as conditions become dryer.

## Blood Detectors

Piranhas can detect blood and are attracted to the tiniest bit of it in the water, so stay out of the water if you have any open cuts or if you are menstruating. If you have recently handled raw meat (e.g. have been gutting fish), this will also attract unwanted attention.

## Good Vibrations

Try to disturb the water as little as possible, and don't make any noise. Piranhas are sensitive to the finest vibrations, and if you thrash around and splash the piranhas will be alerted to your presence and may strike. Human attacks are most common in places where lots of people bathe at the same time.

# 47. Go Whoring in Tangier :

If swearing, cursing, drinking, and whoring are your thing, head over to Tangier, a legendary town on the coast of northern Morocco, and one of the

oldest in North Africa. William Burroughs hung out here with Jack Kerouac and other beat writers, and everyone else from Truman Capote to Henry Matisse has enjoyed its hospitality. Mark Twain endorsed it at the end of *The Innocents Abroad*: "I would seriously recommend to the Government of the United States that when a man commits a crime so heinous that the law provides no adequate punishment for it, they make him Consul-General to Tangier."

## Whore Guides

The scene in Tangier isn't as outrageous as it was in its heyday in the 1950s, but there is still plenty of debauchery. As soon as you leave the airport, train station, or ferry, you will be inundated with locals offering to be your tour guide. If you are feeling reckless, ask one of them to take you to the nearest brothel. If you don't want their help, say, *"laa, shukran"* ("no, thanks" in Arabic) and stride away purposefully.

## Nightlife

The nightlife in Tangier is quite depressing, but go into any bar or one of the many nightclubs and just about every Moroccan woman is a prostitute (even the ones who just look like prostitutes). The music is not at all like you'd hear in a club back home: this is classical Arabic music, improvized around various melody lines, and sounds like a cross between symphonic and Indian string music.

If you want gay sex, most of the tourist guides will try to procure you prostitutes of both sexes, so you won't be short on offers. Men and women will also approach you in restaurants (even good ones) and offer their services.

## Stay Sober

Don't get too drunk, as you'll need to keep your wits about you to avoid being ripped off or robbed, and drunkenness is frowned upon in this Muslim country (many establishments don't offer alcohol).

## Haggle

Be prepared to negotiate. When buying a carpet in Tangier you can usually haggle the price down to an eighth of the asking price. It's the same with personal services. Be sure to practice safe sex; Tangier has the one of the highest rates of HIV-positive sex workers in the world.

# 48. Have a Kidney Transplant in the Philippines:

During the last decade, the Philippines was transplant tourists's number one destination (other hot spots include China, Pakistan, Egypt, and Colombia), and as many as 500 wealthy foreigners visited the country to buy a kidney cheaply from an impoverished citizen.

## Government Crackdown

In 2008, the government changed the law on the sale of organs, and it is now illegal for foreigners to have transplant surgery in the country, unless they are related to Filipino citizens by blood. The Philippines still remains one of the world's cheapest places for wealthy foreign patients wanting to buy a new kidney though, but now if you get caught you face up to twenty years in prison and a fine of up to 2 million pesos (approximately $45,000).

# One Kidney Island

Procure the organ through one of the many brokers who trawls the slums of Manila and the provinces looking for potential donors. One area of Manila has earned the nickname "One Kidney Island" because so many of its inhabitants have sold a kidney. The brokers charge up to $1,500 per transplant and often put up the donors in safe houses or hotels for months until a suitable recipient can be found.

The way it used to work was that you could buy an organ and then the hospital would classify the transaction as a donation. You paid the hospital about $50,000 while a kidney cost you between $2,000 and $10,000 (an enormous sum for a poor family). The hospitals were only supposed to allow ten percent of their transplant patients to be foreigners, but in practice nearly 60 percent of hospitals were exceeding their quota and breaking Health Department guidelines.

Today, you can still have the surgery, but kidney donations are now monitored by a new regulatory body, so you will either have to pay large bribes, or have underground surgery, which brings a higher risk of complications.

# 49. Join the Foreign Legion:

Lost your job, your home, your marriage? Looking for a life of adventure à la Beau Geste? Nowadays you have to join under a declared identity, so you can no longer hide from your criminal past by becoming a Legionnaire. However, you can run away from everything else (apart from sand, sunburn, and singing). You must assume a new Legionnaire name when you join, but you can revert to your old name after a year if you so wish.

## How to Enlist

You can only enlist in mainland France. You must sign up for a minimum of five years and whatever your marital status, you will enlist as a single man. Next comes Preselection in one of the various recruiting offices throughout France (Paris, Aubagne, Lille, Nantes, Strasbourg, Bordeaux, Lyon, Marseille, Nice, Perpignan, and Toulouse). This is followed by Selection, and a 15-week instruction program.

nº: 23458403

26 NOV. 1998

Jamaïca

## Preselection

Preselection lasts one to three days. You will be interviewed to confirm your reasons for enlisting; you must provide valid ID, fill out lots of forms, and pass an initial medical examination.

## Selection

Selection lasts for ten days and takes place in Aubagne near Marseille. It includes personality and psychotechnical tests, logic tests, physical fitness tests, further motivation and security checks, and a more thorough medical check-up. You can also expect detailed background checks via Interpol.

## Instruction Program

Basic training lasts for four weeks and is physically tough and extremely stressful psychologically—not least is it all being in French and there's lots of singing and marching. You must also learn to recite from memory the Legion's code of honor. And sing—did we mention the singing? You'll be in a group with twenty-nine other recruits and you will all be systematically broken down as individuals and reassembled as an elite combat choir with unparalleled *esprit de cours*. They teach you a bit about weapons too (you are issued a FAMAS— *Fusil d'Assaut de la Manufacture d'Armes de Saint-Étienne*—the standard combat assault rifle of the French military) as well as several tins of throat lozenges.

If you pass, you will graduate wearing the prized *Képi Blanc* (white cap). Then you must complete an additional eleven weeks of training and singing before being assigned to your regiment.

After three years of service, you can apply for French citizenship. If you are wounded in active service, you can apply under *Français par le sang versé* (French by spilled blood).

# 50. Street Race in Malaysia:

Street racing is illegal in Malaysia, but that doesn't stop an estimated 200,000 young men from cruising the streets most evenings in their modified cars or sucky little motorcycles in search of an adrenalin rush. If you want to join the scene, buy a scooter or an old Malaysian banger, and see how quickly you can wedge yourself under a truck.

## Mat Rempit

If you race your car or crappy little *kapcai* (scooter) on the street, you are known as *Mat Rempit* in Malay. The root of the term lies in the combination of the expression "ramp the throttle" and the noise made by a two-stroke engine. To impress your girlfriend, you should spend most of your free time performing pointless modifications on your vehicle to squeeze a bit more power from your pathetic piece of junk, and make the exhaust sound less like a hairdryer.

Mat Rempit like to show off (and distinguish themselves from pizza delivery boys) by performing stunts such as the "superman" (head and shoulders at handlebar height, body flat, and one leg cocked on the back of the seat); "scorpion" (stand on the seat with one leg during a wheelie); "sailboat" (stand on the seat and steer with the feet); and *"wikang"* (front wheelie). These efforts are based on the principle that the more stupid the stunt, the more attention is diverted away from your ridiculous bike.

## Cilok Racing

*Cilok* is racing a scooter while weaving in an out of moving and stationery traffic (optional: then posting a video on YouTube of you reaching the speed limit while going downhill with a tailwind).

## Car Racing

Most racers are low-paid or unemployed, so they don't have much money to spend on their cars. Most drive something home-grown or Japanese like a boxy first-generation Proton Douchebag, a small hatchback Daihatsu R-Tard, or a fifteen-year-old Nissan Pantyliner.

## Routes

Recently the police have clamped down on illegal racing, but on weekend nights you'll still find a meet in many of the city centers (Kuala Lumpur, Selangor, Johor Bahru), or check out the drift racing on hill roads such as Bukit Tinggi or Teluk Bahang in Penang. Even watching street races is illegal, so if the police arrive hit the gas and speed away as quickly as your 50cc engine will allow.

# 51. Go Gay in Uganda:

Going gay in Uganda is a riot—or at least, that's what you'd cause if you came out in this beautiful country with otherwise warm and friendly people. Physical affection and contact between guys is commonplace; here men walk down the street holding hands. There is nothing you can't do to show your affection for another man: touch his leg, rub his arm, pat him on the butt, but being openly gay is likely to get you beaten up and imprisoned for up to seven years. Gay women fly completely under the radar because, like most patriarchal cultures, lesbianism is treated as myth.

## The Missionary Legacy

The people in Uganda are open and welcoming, but they just don't believe homosexuality exists in their country. It is strictly taboo and the consensus is that it was brought into the country by the *muzungus*—whites or foreigners. Even the current president Yoweri Museveni has denounced homosexuality in these terms.

Homosexuality was always there, of course, but white missionaries and colonialists imported their religion which vilified it and made it a sin. Far from bringing homosexuality with them, the whites were responsible for stamping it out (or rather, forcing it underground). Some religious and political fanatics in Uganda are lobbying to bring in a life sentence for anyone openly practicing homosexuality.

## Macho Men

Ugandan men are far from the macho brutes you might expect in a country that is supposed to be homophobic to its core. And if you choose to be effeminate, you go girl—it is perfectly acceptable here. Ugandan men exhibit a wide range of so-called "masculine" and "feminine" traits. It is not unusual for a man to throw a tantrum akin to a spoiled six-year-old girl who didn't get the Barbie she wanted.

## Get a Girlfriend

Most gay men here get a girlfriend or wife and use them as a cover (or "beard") to draw suspicion away from their true sexual orientation. If you are white, you are more likely to be viewed with suspicion if you check out other men, but no one will mind too much so long as you keep smiling. Cruising— even other *muzungus*—is quite dangerous, since it is so easy to misinterpret physical signals in Uganda.

## The Kampala Scene

There is a very small underground gay scene, mostly in the capital Kampala. However, you won't find any gay clubs; although, you may get a few guys dancing around you if you are an enthusiastic dancer. Watch out, as they could just be intrigued to see a foreigner break it down, rather than looking to get you into the sack.

# 52. Break into a Panda Reserve:

There are only an estimated 1,000 giant pandas left in the wild, and they are among the most threatened large mammals in the world. So you really don't have the time to wait for the red tape to clear on your request to visit a panda reserve. By the time all your paperwork is processed, you are approved, and you get to the top of the waiting list, pandas may have gone the way of the dodo.

## Where Have All the Pandas Gone?

Besides the fact that humans slaughtered pandas for thousands of years, the black-and-white bears really aren't doing much to help their species. First, despite the fact that they are really carnivores, modern pandas have become such fussy eaters that they only eat bamboo shoots, and not any old shoots either—only one specific type. Also, their digestive system, which is crying out for flesh, can only digest about two percent of the bamboo, and the rest of it passes through. So besides starving themselves, they don't really have any energy to waste having sex.

On the topic of reproduction, the male has an unfeasibly small penis, while the female has a gargantuan vulva, so they aren't well matched. Also, the females are so stupid that the first time they give birth they beat the living crap out of their offspring because they have never seen a baby panda before. Truly, if they didn't look so cute, they'd have been allowed to die out decades ago.

## Panda Reserves

To see a panda in the wild, you will need to travel to China. The Chinese government, along with various wildlife organizations, has set up panda reserves in an attempt to try and save the species. However, access to these areas is extremely limited and the reserves are well patrolled.

If you are willing to risk it all though, your best bet is to head to the Sichuan Giant Panda Sanctuaries in the southwest Sichuan province of China. The Sanctuaries are made up of seven nature reserves and nine scenic parks, with the Wolong National Nature Reserve housing 150 pandas. The large panda population makes this your best option. A stream runs through the Wolong Valley where the reserve is located. Try and find an entry point to the stream that lies outside the reserve's watchful eye. Under the cover of darkness, paddle down the stream and into the reserve.

## Alternatives

Go to the zoo. The zoos in San Diego, Atlanta, and Washington, D.C. all have pandas. Slip the security guard a hundred bucks and may be he'll let you sleep next to the glass.

# 53. Insult the Thai Royal Family:

In places like the UK, there are old and ridiculous laws on the statute books—such as the one that says sticking a stamp upside down on an envelope is treason—but no one takes them seriously. You could take a dump or burn a bank note outside Buckingham Palace and you wouldn't raise an eyebrow. But in Thailand, expressing negative opinions of the monarchy can get you sent to prison for a maximum of fifteen years.

## Lèse Majesté

The *lèse majesté* law in Thailand is the most strictly enforced in the world. The Thai Constitution warns: "The King shall be enthroned in a position of revered worship and shall not be violated. No person shall expose the King to any sort of accusation or action." The country's criminal code says: "Whoever defames, insults, or threatens the King, Queen or the Heir-apparent, shall be punished with imprisonment of three to fifteen years." It doesn't go into greater detail about what form "defames" and "insults" might take, so the law is open to a very wide interpretation.

## Royal Fallibility

The impetus to punish dissenters does not come from the King. In fact, he has publicly expressed his discomfort about the law: "Actually, I must also be criticized. I am not afraid if the criticism concerns what I do wrong, because then I know." He has even admitted his own fallibility: "The King can do wrong." However, the military zealously enforces the law and politicians use lèse majesté as a weapon to eliminate their opponents.

## Flying Princess

You don't even have to "insult" the royal family on Thai soil to break the law. In 1995, Frenchman Lech Tomasz Kisiele-wicz allegedly made a disparaging remark about a Thai princess while on board a Thai Airways flight. He was flying over international waters at the time, but was arrested as soon as the plane touched down in Bangkok. He was imprisoned for two weeks and was only released after writing a grovelling letter of apology to the King.

## Verisimilitude

More recently, Australian author Harry Nicolaides was arrested at a Bangkok airport while waiting for a plane home to Melbourne because of three lines in his self-published book *Verisimilitude*. The lines alluded to the romantic life of an unspecified Thai crown prince. Before publication, Harry thought he had protected himself by sending copies of the manuscript to the National Library, the Thai Ministry of Culture, the Thai Ministry of Foreign Affairs, and the Bureau of the Royal Household for approval. He received no reply, so he assumed all was well. At his trial, he pleaded guilty to the offense of lèse majesté and was sentenced to three years in prison, but he was released after six months. Until then, the book had sold just seven copies.

## Banknotes and Newspapers

If you drop a Thai coin or banknote on the floor, remember that it contains the image of the King's head. Pick it up carefully; don't trap it with your foot to stop it rolling or blowing away, as this is equivalent to stomping on the King. Likewise, don't roll up a newspaper that features his photo to swat a fly, or use for toilet paper.

# 54. Swim the Rio Grande:

The Rio Grande (or *Río Bravo* as it is called in Mexico) is 1,885 miles long and the fourth longest river in the United States. It is the natural border between Texas and the Mexican states of Chihuahua, Coahuila, Nuevo León, and Tamaulipas. Each year 1.5 million illegal immigrants successfully make it into the United States from Mexico, and many still swim the Rio Grande the old-fashioned way.

## Beaten Path Effect

Cross in a rural area away from the city, but don't fall victim to the "beaten path effect." Profilers of border crossing patterns have found that many cross where others have successfully crossed before. This makes you more vulnerable to capture, since a popular and successful crossing place quickly turns into a well-patrolled one. Select a crossing point that is less well known.

## Cross at Peak Time

Crossing at a peak place reduces your chances of success; however, crossing at a peak time increases it. Most illegal border crossings take place from Thursday to Sunday, and Saturday is the busiest day of the week. Monday is the quietest. It's a numbers game: if you cross on Monday, when the ratio of immigrants to border patrol guards is smallest, you are more likely to get caught than if you cross on Saturday when the border patrol resources are overstretched. The two peak times of day are 10:00 A.M. to 2:00 P.M., and from 8:00 P.M. to 10:00 P.M.

## Location

Crossing the Rio Grande is most dangerous during times of high or fast water flow. It is safer to cross a wide body of slow moving water than a short fast-flowing stretch, no matter how tempting the short distance may appear. Choose a location where the water is shallowest (some places you only need to wade, rather than swim) and slow moving. It is worth calling on the services of a "coyote" (an illegal crossing guide), who will house you in a back alley shanty (a "stash house") until nightfall, and then lead you and a group of other hopefuls to the crossing point.

## Take Cover

Make sure that there is good cover on both banks. Find
a place where there is plenty of *carrizo* (river cane). Also,
if the south side bank is significantly higher than the north
side, you can scan for border patrol vehicles on the U.S. side
before you take the plunge.

# 55. Be a Drug Runner:

Being a drug runner isn't as easy as it was during the '60s, when criminals were way ahead of the game and airport surveillance was in its infancy. Now with a very real prospect of getting caught, you've got to weigh your fee against the possibility of spending twenty years rotting in a foreign jail, with cockroaches nesting in your ears, and a cellmate who wants to re-enact some of the missing scenes from *Milk*.

## Body Packing

Drug mules who carry merchandise inside their own bodies (stomach, rectum, vagina, etc.) are called "body packers"; "swallowers," well . . . swallow. It's less risky than keeping it in your carry-on in terms of getting caught (although your body may still be X-rayed by airport security), but potentially much more dangerous to your health. Don't swallow hashish as the fee won't compensate for the risk. You can carry around two pounds of Class A drugs in your stomach. The old-fashioned method is to fill condoms to make little pellets, and then swallow them. Later, you use laxatives like diphenoxylate or loperamide to get them to come out quickly. Enemas are also recommended if you've shoved any drugs up your ass.

The dangers are considerable: if you suddenly develop acute anxiety, dilated pupils, a rapid heartbeat, and can't stop sweating, the condom has split and is leaking inside you. You have two choices: check yourself into the ER where you will be treated for a drug overdose, and then arrested (and your handlers will probably want to kill you), or sweat it out alone and pray you don't die from an overdose. Just remember, sometimes your handlers won't wait for you to pass the drugs out naturally—they will kill and cut you open.

If everything goes according to plan, you'll be paid a fee related to the number of pellets you have swallowed—about $8,000 per kilo maximum—plus your air fare and hotel expenses. The cartel will sell the drugs for five or six times this price and the street value in a city like New York could be forty times your cut.

## Know Your Back Story

If you're supposed to be on vacation, have vacation plans, know where you are going to stay, and have the right amount of luggage. Dress appropriately (i.e. don't be the only person wearing casual clothes on a mid-afternoon flight full of suited business travelers). Don't board or disembark from the plane first or last (this is what drug mules usually do). Don't be overly cooperative with customs officials.

## Smuggling Routes

Smuggling around Europe or from Panama into the United States is preferable to Asia, where many countries have mandatory death penalties for anyone caught with even the smallest amounts of drugs. For example, in Singapore the death sentence is mandatory for trafficking in more than 15 grams of heroin, 30 grams of cocaine, or 500 grams of cannabis, and your family won't even be notified that you've been hung until after your death. Avoid China, Thailand, Brazil, India, and Saudi Arabia as well—you don't even want to go to prison in these countries, let alone die. The best place to make your runs are the Scandinavian countries where, if you get caught, you'll be sent to a humane facility where you will be fed on wild pheasant and caviar and can get yourself a college education.

# 56. Hitchhike from LA to NYC:

Just how crazy, optimistic, or suicidal do you have to be to hitchhike today? Hello—are you living in the '80s? Actually, it's not all that bad—if you know what you're doing. However, if just waiting for a bus makes you bored, then hitching will likely kill you.

1. Before you start, buy some maps, so you can figure out which rides are actually taking you closer to your destination rather than to some crazy trucker's lock-up.

2. Wear bright clean clothing so that drivers can see you, but not so bright that drivers think that you are a nutcase (or French).

3. Don't hitch from the center of town; get a bus to the edge of town.

4. Choose a hitching spot where you can be seen clearly from a long way off, and where drivers can stop safely and legally. Hitching on the highway is illegal, but you'll have to weigh the benefit of traffic flow versus getting arrested.

5. It's safer to travel with a companion, but being part of a trio won't get you very far at all. You'll get picked up mostly by solitary male drivers in empty cars, and some females. Also, try to avoid squeezing into a full car where you're outnumbered.

6. If you have waited an hour, start walking in the direction you want to go. Sometimes it's even better to accept a short ride in the wrong direction to a better pick-up point than wait in a bad place. Be prepared to do a lot of walking and stay cheerful. If you treat a lift as a bonus, you'll have a better mental attitude.

7. Pack plenty of food and water, as you never know where your next rest stop will be—and gas stations are expensive.

8. Don't give the driver your final destination; this leaves you an excuse to be dropped off if you feel uncomfortable.

9. A highway rest area is a good place to ask around for a lift while people are refuelling their cars. It avoids the illegality of hitching on the highway itself. Expect plenty of rejections, but it does give both parties more of a chance to size each other up. However, many hitchhikers avoid rest areas because there's a greater risk of being picked up by a serial mugger or rapist. The more commercial rest areas on toll roads are probably your safest option.

10. Right before highway on-ramps are good places to hitch, but if you do it on truck stop property you can be thrown off for trespassing. Many spots before on-ramps are also bus stops, making hitching illegal.

11. Hitching at night is very difficult and more dangerous. Try to travel during the day unless it's an emergency.

12. Some hitchers swear by big cardboard signs; others hate them. Writing a nearby destination can get you a succession of short lifts, which is better than staying put. Occasionally, if you hold your sign upside down, you may attract a pity ride. The less you write the better (e.g. "NYC" not "New York City"—the driver only has a moment to read).

13. Sit in the front passenger seat: back seats may have child locks. Keep your bag on your lap, so if you need to bail, your belongings aren't locked in the trunk.

14. Keep your money in your groin, not your sock. If you get robbed, the sock will be the first place a mugger will look.

15. If in doubt, turn down the ride.

# 57. Join the Mile High Club:

The MHC is always open to new members. There is no dress code, membership fee, or stuffy protocol; in fact, the only entry requirement is engaging in sexual intercourse on board an airplane while it is in flight, at least 1 mile (5,280 feet) above the ground.

## Founding Members

The founders of the MHC are thought to be the pilot Lawrence Sperry and Mrs. Waldo Polk, while on board a Curtiss Flying Boat en route to New York in November 1916. Sperry engaged the auto pilot which he designed himself, and got to work with the married woman.

## Legal Implications

You can be arrested for public indecency if your coupling takes place in view of other passengers. If you get it on in the toilet or in one of the double beds in the new Airbus A380, then the legality depends on the airline you are flying with, your departure and destination points, and which country you were over flying at the time.

In 1999, two married strangers in business class on an American Airlines flight from Dallas to Manchester were arrested for performing sex acts in view of other passengers. After downing two bottles of wine and several glasses of cognac and port, the woman stripped to her underwear halfway through the in-flight movie when the lights were dimmed and the couple refused to stop despite repeated requests from the flight crew, even after the lights had been switched on. They were arrested by Manchester police upon landing and both lost their jobs. At the time, the woman worked for Nortel Networks, whose TV advertising slogan was "come together." Sometimes you can be too on-message.

## Celebrity Mile-highers

Virgin Atlantic Airways owner Richard Branson claims to have joined the MHC when he was 19 by having sex with a married woman in the toilet (he didn't know she was married at the time). Ralph Fiennes is alleged to have had sex with flight attendant Lisa Roberston in a business class lavatory on board a Qantas flight bound for Mumbai in February 2007. She lost her job and Fiennes has made no comment.

## Charter a Flight

Part of the thrill of having sex in the air, apart from the heightened sensations many report due to the reduced air pressure, is the illicit nature of the act, and the chance of getting caught. However, several companies offer private charter flights for the risk-averse who want to get it on in the air.

# 58. Land a Plane in Red Square:

At around 7.00 P.M. on May 28, 1987, nineteen-year-old German political activist Mathias Rust landed a light aircraft on a bridge next to St. Basil's Cathedral, and then taxied to within 100 yards of Red Square. If you want to recreate Rust's historic feat, you'll need an extraordinary amount of luck, just like him. Air defense systems are more sophisticated than twenty years ago, and post-9/11, rogue aircrafts are certain to be shot down. But what the hell: here's how to follow his route in five easy steps:

1. Rent a plane in Hamburg, Germany. Rust rented a Reims Cessna F172—a four-seat, single-engine, fixed-wing plane, and the most successful mass produced light aircraft in history. Good choice. Other options include the Piper PA-28 Cherokee, the Grumman American AA-5 series, or the Diamond DA40 (which is the most attractive ride—the others look a bit boxy).

2. In the morning, fly to Finland and refuel at Helsinki-Malmi Airport. Ask air traffic control for clearance to

fly to Stockholm in Sweden, but instead, turn off all your communication equipment and head east.

3. At some point along your route, air traffic control may think you've crashed and will go about starting a search and rescue mission. This is costly; Rust was charged $100,000 for his.

4. Cross the Baltic coastline in Estonia and then turn towards Moscow. By now the Russian military should have assigned you a combat number, and several surface-to-air missile (SAM) divisions start have you in their sights. Rust was lucky that permission to engage was withheld. Post-9/11 you won't be.

5. If by a miracle you are still alive, look out for interceptor planes. If they don't shoot you down, land near Staraya Russa, an old Russian town fifty miles south of Veliky Novgorod. Change your clothes and eat some sandwiches, and then make the final push to Moscow. Pray that the Central Air Defence System has been turned off for maintenance, and you should reach Red Square by early evening. You can try landing in the Square, but you'll kill lots of pedestrians.

## Do Your Time

Rust was sentenced to four years in a Soviet labor camp, but he actually served only 432 days in an interrogation prison because the KGB couldn't guarantee his safety. He was locked up in a thirteen square-yard cell for twenty-two hours each day and it hit him "so hard—much harder than I had thought." However, you'll be lucky to reach Step 4, so anything else is a bonus.

# 59. Ride the Subway for Free:

New York City's public transportation system is one of the oldest and biggest in the world. Every day more than eight million people ride the bus and subway systems. It's quite cheap, too, but it's better if you can ride for free.

## Token Sucking

Let's take a moment to look back fondly at the good ol' days of token operated subway turnstiles. You paid for your token, and then dropped it through the slot on top of the gate, and through you went. It was easy for a "token sucker" to press his lips around the filthy slot, where thousands of dirty hands had been, and suck a token back out of the machine. The downside was the germs you ingested, but then you could ride the subway for free or sell the token for a dollar. Happy days. Not so any more.

## Fold Your Metrocard Along the T

Metrocards can be folded in such a way that they unlock the turnstiles and you get to ride the subway for free, even when there is insufficient credit on the card. Fold the card along the T of the word "Metrocard" and then swipe it. You may need to do this a couple times. If it doesn't work, move on or you'll attract attention (and if you get caught you may get prosecuted for criminal possession of a forged instrument). Most people don't bother trying because word got around that it doesn't work anymore when it became too popular and that there was a clamp down. Not so, so get folding and swiping.

## Jump the Turnstiles

You risk a $60 to $100 fine, but most of the guards are so fat they can't run very far. If you get chased, make sure you don't fall on the track and get your legs run over. Having your mangled feet amputated just isn't worth saving $2.

## Ride Around All Day

If you pay to get on one line, and then change trains, you can ride around the subway system all day for the price of one ticket. Now that's value for money. Also, Metrocards give you a free transfer within two hours of the ride, so if you travel to your destination on the bus, you can ride back again on the subway for free within two hours.

## Get Ordained?

There's an episode of *Friends* where Joey says that he got ordained online and that he can now ride the subway for free. It's not true.

# 60. Survive a Train Bombing:

You're sitting sleepily on the subway psyching yourself up for another day in the office. Suddenly a young man wearing a bulky jacket and sweating profusely boards your car clutching his chest and muttering some sort of mantra. You are witnessing the last moments of a suicide bomber. Is there anything you can do, or is it too late?

## Sweet Spot

The safest spot on a train is near the back, away from the entrance. If you can, select a less-crowded car towards the rear of the train (a bomber will always try to pick a crowded one to inflict the most casualties). In a crowded compartment, it is safer to sit than stand because you are less exposed to shrapnel and head wounds.

n°: 23458403
26 NOV. 1998
Jamaïca

## Put Distance Between You and the Bomber

If the bomber is in your car, run away from him. The explosion will create a pressure wave, so the more distance you can put between you and him, the better your chances of survival, even if it is just a few feet. After the explosion, do not approach the bomber or the bomber's remains. There may be undetonated or partially detonated explosives or secondary devices present.

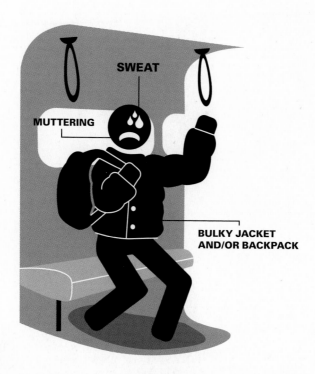

SWEAT

MUTTERING

BULKY JACKET AND/OR BACKPACK

## Keep Away from the Walls

During a pressure blast, shrapnel and debris will not bounce off walls like a ball; they roll along them like a wave. If possible, do not stand within an arm's length of walls, as broken glass and other projectiles will be most concentrated in these zones.

## Prepare for Derailment

If the explosion happens in another car, keep your shoes on, remove your glasses and any sharp objects (keys, pens, etc.) from your pockets, and assume the crash position with your head between your knees. If the explosion is in your car, you will most likely be injured and in shock. Evacuate immediately and expect a follow-up bombing.

## First Aid

Lift bleeding limbs above your heart and apply pressure to any bleeding wounds with your hand. If you are too badly injured to move, stay as immobile as possible to prevent further injury, until help arrives.

If you are hidden from sight, do not struggle, as this could make your injuries worse. Do not waste energy yelling, as this may cause you to inhale toxic fumes and dust. Clap or tap on something to alert rescuers.

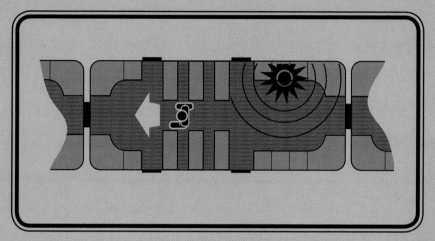

# 61. Swim with Sharks:

There are few killers more efficient than the great white shark, a carnage machine that grows up to twenty feet long and 5,000 lbs in weight, with teeth sharper than a scalpel blade. It is at the top of its food chain, so the moment you get into the water with one you become prey. In the last fifteen years, there have been approximately 900 shark attacks of which 100 have been fatal. If you want to swim with sharks and survive, pay attention:

**1. Florida has the highest incidence of shark attacks in the world, followed by Australia, South Africa, Brazil, and Hawaii.**

**2. Some species of shark come inshore to feed at dawn, dusk, and during the night, so avoid the water at these times in high-risk areas.**

**3. Sharks are attracted to splashing and activity in the water, so try to swim smoothly and keep pets and children out of the water, as they are always splashing around. Surfing appears to be the biggest risk factor; you are twice as likely to be attacked while surfing than while diving. The reason for this is that the activity on the surface of the water attracts the sharks.**

4. Don't swim with an open wound. Sharks can detect blood and other bodily fluids in minute concentrations. If you are bleeding or have an open wound, stay out of the water, and don't pee in your wetsuit when there are sharks around.

5. A shark like a great white will take an exploratory nibble then come back for the kill. If you can flee after the first nibble, you will escape with your life.

6. A shark's eyesight can pick out contrast well, so avoid wearing high contract clothing, or shiny objects such as jewelry.

7. Stay away from people who are fishing, and don't swim if you've recently handled dead fish or other dead animals like if you've been gutting fish.

8. Don't swim alone. If you get attacked, your friends can pick up the pieces and bring them to shore.

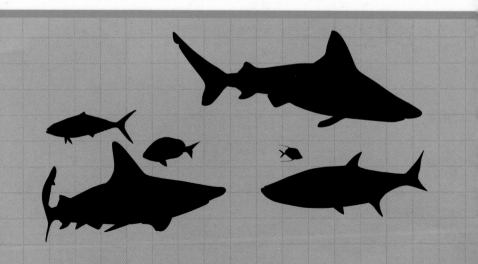

# 62. Track Down the Most Poisonous Animals:

When normal people go on safari they want to see the Big Five: lion, leopard, elephant, rhinoceros, and African buffalo. But where's the danger in that? An intrepid traveler like you should use the following checklist when planning your wild safari. Here's a list of the world's most poisonous animals—much cooler than the Big Five. Don't get too close though; you might be heading home in the cargo hold.

## Poison Dart Frog

It has *poison* in its *name*. This brightly colored little creature is definitely no Kermit. However, one touch and you'll certainly be feeling green. In order to see one in the wild, you'll need to travel to the rainforests of Central and South America. Ones in captivity do not secret poison (at least not much) since the toxic chemical emission is actually a build up of the poisonous chemicals from their prey.

## Deathstalker Scorpion

To find this dangerous creature, head to the deserts of North Africa or the Middle East. Besides being yellow and relatively lightly armored, it's not a typical scorpion species as its sting is very poisonous and very painful. If stung, the neurotoxins it releases will cause an intense pain followed by an agonizing fever before you finally slip into a coma.

## Blue-ringed Octopus

You will need to go underwater to find this member of the Poisonous Five. And being about the size of a ping-pong ball with the ability to camouflage itself (the vibrant blue rings on its skin aren't visible unless provoked), it is going to be a hard one to locate. Be very cautious as you check the coral and rock crevices for this tiny wonder. There is no known antidote for the poison contained in the animal's saliva. One bite and you better hope you're near a respirator because you will need assistance breathing until the toxins work out of your system, which usually takes about twenty-four hours. If you're still up for the challenge, its habitat is shallow Pacific tide pools, anywhere from Australia to Japan.

## Inland Taipan

All this snake wants is to be left alone. Unfortunately, as the world's most poisonous land snake, it has found its way on to the list. Found in the heart of Australia, its scales change color depending on the season so you will need to be mindful of what month it is before you go searching for this serpent. If it is winter, you should be on the lookout for the dark brown scales. If it is summer, you want to watch for a snake that is more of an olive-green. The bite from an inland taipan contains enough venom to kill 100 humans, but as mentioned, it is a rather docile creature. So look; don't poke it with a stick.

## Sydney Funnel-web Spider

Stay Down Under to catch a glimpse of the last of the Poisonous Five. The Sydney funnel-web spider is native to—you guessed it—Sydney, Australia. Only males contain the venom component that is dangerous to your nervous system. But they are also the ones who leave the burrow in order to find a mate, and can sometimes wander into homes. They can get up to about three inches and length and typically have a glossy bluish-black to dark plum color. If you do end up spotting one, stay away. This species of arachnid is quite aggressive and will attack.

# 63. Break 200 MPH on the Autobahn:

There are few places on the planet where you can drive a passenger car as fast as you want; the German Autobahn is one of them. However, there are only a handful of production cars in the world capable of breaking the magic 200 MPH barrier.

## Buy Some Wheels

You need to spend a minimum of $120,000 to buy a car that will break 200 MPH, and then more like $150,000 if you want something classy like a Porsche Carrera Turbo. A cheaper alternative would be to spend about $50,000 on the car and hundreds of hours (and dollars) in the workshop to adapt something like a Corvette.

There's a world of difference between doing 180 and 200 because the wind resistance increases exponentially, and you need a third more power to gain ten percent more speed. The first production car that could exceed 200 MPH was the Ferrari F40, launched in 1987. Next came RUF's 469 bhp CTR "Yellowbird," and then the McLaren F1 hit 242 MPH in 1993, which no one could beat for a decade. Now we are entering another golden age with speeds heading towards 300 MPH in the next few years. Today, a Bugatti Veyron will comfortably reach 250 MPH and still feel very stable, but it well set you back well over a million dollars.

## Hit the Road

Before your attempt, familiarize yourself with a flat, dry stretch of Autobahn because even the slightest curve can become a challenge when you're speeding. Also, travel in the early morning, mid-morning, or at night when the roads are quietest. Get someone else to check the speedometer because if you take your eye off the road for a second you will travel blindly 293 feet (you travel a mile every 18 seconds). If some-one a quarter of a mile away pulled out into your lane doing 50 MPH, you'd hit them in less than six seconds if you didn't ease off the gas and apply the brake.

More than half of the German Autobahn has no speed restric-tions, so you've got about 6,835 miles to play around with. The Autobahn is actually safer than U.S. highways because drivers have to be 18 before they can get behind the wheel, the test-ing is more rigorous, the left lane is only used for passing, the road surface is better quality, and, let's be honest, Ger-mans drive better and safer cars.

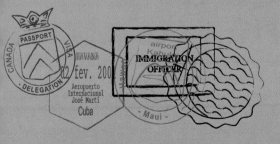

# 64. Enter the Houses of Parliament Wearing a Suit of Armor:

There's an old British law that makes it an offense to wear a suit of armor in the Houses of Parliament. It's probably something to do with the clanking noise waking up Parliament members. Tom Cruise should have made a movie about this instead of *Mission Impossible III*, since it's a physical, mental, and logistical challenge that far surpasses trying to retrieve a rabbit's foot from a facility in Shanghai.

## Buy a Suit of Armor

An authentic wearable replica of a medieval suit of armor will set you back about $2,000. Buy it online and then have it sent to an address in the UK, so you don't have to bring it on a plane. A generic model will fit a person between 5'7" at 150 lbs to 6'0" at 220 lbs maximum (tighten the adjustable straps to suit). It will be constructed out of 18-gauge carbon steel and will weigh about 50 lbs. Buy a full over-the-collar style chain mail coif for about

$50 to complete the look. Sword is optional, but likely to attract an armed response unit (which in the UK shoots first and evades questions later).

In days of yore, all knights employed a squire to help them get into their armor. Get a friend to be your squire because you won't be able to dress on your own. Have a pee, and put on your armor before you travel to Westminster. Wear some tight fitting sweatpants and a long-sleeved shirt underneath for comfort.

## Getting There

On the London subway, take the District, Circle, or Jubilee lines to Westminster station, or hop on a bus and stop near Parliament Square on Victoria Street opposite the Houses of Parliament.

## Enter the Houses of Parliament

Free tours are held throughout the year for UK residents, who must apply through their local Member of Parliament or a Lord, or they can pay for a tour during the summer recess. Overseas visitors can only tour Parliament during the summer recess, but they can attend debates throughout the year (wait in line at St. Stephen's entrance). Try to avoid hot, sunny days, as you may get heat stroke while waiting in your armor, especially if eight police officers are pinning you to the floor. If you manage to evade capture, there's a fair chance that you will set off the metal detectors. If so, don't try to bluff; just make a mad dash for the Members' Lobby.

# 65. Find the Perfect Thai Bride:

If you are lonely, reaching retirement age, and want a hot Thai bride who will cook, clean, and treat you like a god, then jump on the next plane to Bangkok, where Western men (even ugly, broke, old ones like you) are seen as a good catch. You'll never have to put up with a demanding Western woman again.

## What's in It for Her?

Even if you don't have much money, you still offer a chance for your bride to see the world, and you're probably richer than most Thai men. Rightly or wrongly, Thai women view Western men as kinder and more faithful than Thai men, who often have a mistress on the side. Unless you are the same age, accept that she is probably not in love with you, but is attracted by what you can offer her. Do you really think she'd shack up with a blue collar pensioner if she had better prospects at home?

## What's in It for You?

It is statistically proven that being in a relationship is healthier than being single. Thai women are often beautiful, thin, and very feminine. They have a reputation for being devoted and subservient, and expert at making their men feel worshipped. Your new bride will certainly live up to these expectations until you get her home, when you'll discover that she is actually a lot more strong willed and demanding than she first appeared.

## How to Find True Love

The language barrier can be just that—an obstacle to really getting to know each other. Don't assume that your dream princess will bother to learn English when you get home. Trying to communicate when neither of you share a common language can quickly become a real nuisance.

If you just want a bride, then one of the many online or Bangkok dating agencies will set you up with one no trouble, and you could be going home satisfied within a few days. However, if you want your relationship to last, choose someone the same age as you who shares the same interests and has a similar educational background. If you live and work in Thailand for a year you'll meet Thai women at parties and through friends, just like you would back home. This is more natural than cruising the bars or dating sites; you won't be lacking in female attention using these avenues, but nice Thai girls don't try to find husbands in those ways.

# 66. Smuggle Live Animals:

People love pets. People especially love exotic pets. Help people get what they love by smuggling exotic pets into the country. There's many different ways to get all sorts of animals by those pesky custom offi-cials. You just have to get creative—and be ballsy. Whether you dare to walk through the airport with a monkey posing as a toupee or with a snake coiled around your chest, it's up to you. Exude confidence and you'll be all set . . . right?

Here's a list of some of the most sought-after exotic animals:

1. **PYGMY MARMOSET:** The smallest of all monkeys, it's native to the South American rainforests and could double as a toupee or possible tuft of chest hair if you plan on picking one up and flying it back to the States.

2. **SHINGLEBACK SKINK:** A short-tailed lizard that lives in Australia, its rough skin will cause some issues when you try to shove it down your pants to get it past airport security.

3. KEEL-BILLED TOUCAN: What better way to enjoy your morning Fruit Loops than with a live toucan perched on your kitchen counter? Apparently this is how a lot of people want to start off their days as these exotic birds are in high-demand. Road trip it to Bolivia and purchase one from a street vendor for cheap. Drive back up and sell it for big bucks.

4. SNOW LEOPARD: Head over to the Himalayas and see about coming into ownership of a baby snow leopard. These spotted wild cats can catch quite a price at an illegal exotic pet auction. Take your tabby with you when you head over to Asia, and swap him out with the leopard—hoping your old cat's custom forms work for your new acquisition.

5. ROCK PYTHON: Travel to any African country south of the Sahara and see if you can purchase a rock python from any of the local vendors. You'll most likely be able to pay pennies for the snake that will make you some major scratch back home. In terms of getting home—wrap the snake around your torso and waltz right through security. Just be careful things don't get a little too tight.

# 67. Beat a Metal Detector:

Metal detectors have been a standard fixture in airports since the '60s and within the next ten years they will be replaced by full-body scanners, so get your kicks while you can.

## How Metal Detectors Work

Almost all airport metal detectors use pulse induction (PI). The detector sends out a short but very powerful pulse of electricity which creates a brief magnetic field. By measuring how quickly the magnetic field collapses, the detector can tell whether metal is present. The magnetic field lasts a fraction longer when it encounters metal, similar to the way a sound wave will bounce off a room with metal walls, and cause an echo.

## Asbestos

Some sources claim that it is possible to conceal metal objects in an asbestos sheet, rubber, or concrete. This is supposed to stop the magnetic field from reaching the metal, but since airports also use X-ray machines, these materials would show up as anomalies.

In theory, it ought to be possible to create an electronic device that would cloak metal objects by neutralizing where the magnetic field comes into contact with the metal, but that's CIA stuff, and would take a whole book to explain, even if we knew how. Diplomatic pouches are a much easier low-tech solution to this problem.

## CIA Glass Gun

In the movie *In the Line of Fire*, John Malkovitch makes a gun out of plastic and manages to smuggle it in pieces past a metal detector; in *Die Hard II*, it's a ceramic gun (a fictional "Glock 7"). There has been a lot of buzz surrounding non-metal weapons in the media as well. A story appeared in the *Washington Post* in 1985 entitled "Quaddafi Buying Austrian Plastic Pistol," but currently the technology to make guns out of plastic and ceramics still doesn't exist in the public domain.

It is highly likely that secret hi-tech materials with the strength and functionality of metal have been developed by the military and secret services, or poached from industry—an article in a 1995 issue of *Modern Gun* discussed rumors that the CIA had appropriated a new material developed by General Motors for its exhaust valves. It also talks about a "glass gun" made out of ceramics. However, this is all very hi-tech, so the best you can do is get something like the Glock 17, which when stripped down can only be spotted with special training. Your bullets would have to be non-metal too, unless you conceal them in a rabbit's foot key-ring.

# 68. Free Climb the Eiffel Tower:

POLICE NATIONALE
Aéroport de Paris
26 NOV. 1998
🕸 FRANCE 🕸

The iron tower completed on the Champ de Mars beside the Seine River in Paris in 1889 is one of the most famous manmade objects in the world. During its lifetime, the 1,063 foot structure has been visited by more than 200 million people, making it the most visited monument with an admission fee on the planet. Evidently, if you want to stand out from the crowd, you need to do something unique on your visit—like scale it without ropes.

## Urban Climbing

Who hasn't at some time or other shimmied up a drainpipe when they forgot their house keys? How hard can it be to climb the Eiffel Tower? Read *With Bare Hands*, written by the talented nutcase and "Human Spider," Robert Alain, the most famous and successful free climber in the world. You'll be good to go after gleaning some pointers from his mixture of climbing philosophy ("Man creates his own limitations, but we all have within us the strength to overcome to achieve our goals.") and practical tips, such as carrying a small pouch of chalk to dip your hands in.

## The Ascent

The tower is split into three levels. You can reach the first two by stairs (347 steps to the first level, 327 steps to the second level) and elevators, but the top of the third level is only accessible to the public by elevator, or in your case, free climbing. It will save you 12 Euros—barely enough to buy an overpriced espresso and croissant on the Champs-Elysées—so don't attempt the climb just to save money. You'll get arrested and fined afterwards anyway.

## Tips for Death-Free Urban Climbing

1. Cut your fingernails.

2. Buy some good quality climbing shoes.

3. Don't look down, except when tying your shoelaces.

4. Don't climb when it's wet—surfaces become too slippery.

5. Only climb structures that support a load, not ornamental features.

6. When resting, straighten your arms and lean back.

7. Climb slowly and methodically.

8. Carry some ID or your dentist's phone number for when you get scraped off the sidewalk.

# 69. Eat Road Kill:

When you're on a road trip, there's no cheaper and healthier way to eat while traveling than scraping dead animals off the pavement and cooking them to perfection, just the way you like them.

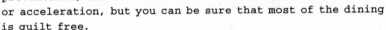

**Five Reasons to Dine**

1. **Even vegetarians should eat road kill**, since the animals lead a happy life in the wild and weren't killed only to be eaten. Some of the deaths are probably preventable, due to driver error or acceleration, but you can be sure that most of the dining is guilt free.

2. **It doesn't cost anything.**

3. **It isn't processed or stuffed full of preservatives, emulsifiers, artificial coloring, growth hormones, antibiotics, and all the other nasties that supermarket meals contain.**

4. **You know where the animal came from**—excellent provenance plus it's fresh (mostly), local, seasonal, and rich in flavor and nutrients.

5. **You can use the skin and fur.**

## Preparation Tips

Only collect intact specimens. If you have to pick up scraps of flesh from all over the road, move on. Don't take the carcass if you suspect that other predators have got to it before you. You may think that you can cut out the bite marks, but it won't stop you from catching something nasty. Avoid animals with dull eyes, bad smell, flies, or maggots.

In the middle of summer, the road kill should be no more than a day old. The best place to collect fresh meat is on roads that you travel on frequently. If the animal wasn't there when you drove past yesterday, then you know it's fresh.

# 70. Clear Airport Security without I.D.:

On domestic flights within the United States, it is possible to board a flight even if you are carrying no ID—no passport, credit card, driver's licence, library card, or electricity bill. All you need to know is the color of your house.

## Save Time

The next time you travel from Chicago to Los Angeles, or wherever, don't bother wasting an hour trying to find your passport, and since your driver's license picture looks absolutely nothing like you, it's likely to earn you a strip search. In fact, it'll be more fun if you leave all identification at home because the Transportation Security Administration agent can now ask you some *really* personal questions.

## Personal Quiz

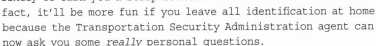

First of all, you'll be asked to fill out a form asking for the standard details, like your social security number, name and address, and date of birth. Then the agent will dial a number and hand the phone over to you. On the other end is another agent who will start off by asking you regular stuff like whether you used to live in New York, or own a red Corvette. Then they'll throw in the curve ball: "What color is your house?" You'd better have an answer ready because everyone knows that, right? The next question might be: "Have you got a swimming pool in your backyard?" or "Is the park behind or in front of your house?" The reason the agent can do this is because he's called up your address on Google Earth.

## Identity Fraud Just Got Easier

This means that stealing someone's identity and using it to travel on a flight is easier than it used to be. The system can correctly identify honest people who are telling the truth about who they are, but it also allows you to use information that is in the public domain (the rest of their personal information you can hack anyway) to strengthen your cover, without having to forge documents. Assuming you've already ordered the ticket using their credit card (details hacked from the Internet), have stolen their social security details from an IRS mainframe, and all their other personal information by looking at Facebook, the final piece of the jigsaw is to bone up on a few details about their immediate neighborhood. Bring some color swatches and you can even show off your new curtains.

# 71. Chase a Giant Tornado:

Tornadoes are some of the most violent and dangerous natural events on earth. Every year in the United States, more than a thousand tornadoes spring up; many of them amount to nothing while others tear across the landscape for hours causing mayhem and destruction. A few really rare tornadoes obliterate whole communities. Next summer, take a three week vacation in the central plains and go storm chasing.

## What Is a Tornado?

Tornadoes are rotating columns of air that extend from the ground to the cumulonimbus clouds in the sky. Warm humid air at ground spins as it rises and meets colder air higher up; combine this with a large rotating thunderstorm ("supercell") overhead and you've got the conditions for a killer tornado. About one in a thousand thunderstorms become supercells, and one in six of those generate a tornado. You need to know a lot about the weather, or hang around with someone who does to stand a chance of getting up close to a tornado, and doing so safely.

## When and Where

In the US, about 40 percent of tornadoes appear in the central plains between March and July. Boulder, Colorado—at the foot of the Rocky Mountains—makes a good base camp because you can see for hundreds of miles across the plains, spot the supercells, and drive right to the action.

## Technology and Experience

Tornado chasers drive around in vans that are packed with antennae and satellite dishes and they have banks of screens, computers, and satellite-linked televisions to help them predict what's happening with the weather. The successful ones are also staffed with incredibly experienced people. You can't just jump in a pick-up and head for the nearest storm clouds because you'll put yourself in extreme danger. Don't chase tornadoes on your own. You'll reduce your odds of seeing one and increase your chances of getting injured.

For your first season, try to hook up with a seasoned storm chaser; they are hard to find, because they are outnumbered by newbies like you. Otherwise, follow one (they hate that)! Another option is to book a packaged "tornado safari" with a tour firm of skilled chasers; these include Silver Lining Tours, Tempest Tours, or Cloud 9 Tours.

# Get Used to Truck-Stop Catering

You will cover hundreds of miles, and the rest of the time you'll be sitting around snacking on truck-stop food waiting for things to kick off. On the road, your biggest dangers aren't tornadoes; they are more mundane threats such as aquaplaning, crashing, or being struck by lightning. Most likely, you won't even see a tornado at all, just lots of rain, hailstones, and Twinkies.

# 72. Swim Down the Amazon:

The Amazon River is the second longest river in the world (after the Nile), but the largest in terms of water volume. Only one person has swam its entire length—Slovenian marathon swimmer, Martin Strel. You could be the second, and, depending on your age, the youngest (Strel was 53). If you're tempted, here is the challenge that you face.

## Find the Source

The most distant source of the Amazon is a glacial stream on a peak called Nevado Mismi in the Peruvian Andes, 18,363 feet above sea level, but the first place from which you can swim is Atalaya in Peru. You will finish in Belem, Brazil, 3,274 miles away. Strel completed the swim in just sixty-six days, from February 1, 2007 to April 7, 2007.

## Preparations

Don't try to swim on your own. You'll need a back-up flotilla of at least three boats and a team of around forty-five people. It's their job to warn you of danger (you'll have your head in

the water), keep you on course (steer away from rocks, etc.),
help you in and out of the water, treat your wounds, feed you,
give you massages, and keep your spirits up. Choose a motto;
Strel's was "I swim for peace, friendship and clean waters."

If you are a fit marathon swimmer, you will already have
warmed up with other river swims, such as the Mississippi,
Danube, or Yangtze, and you'll need to train for at least
eighteen months prior to your swim and put on about forty
extra pounds (you'll lose most of it during the attempt).
You should aim to swim for fourteen hours and an average of
thirty-eight miles each day. Like Strel, you will often be in
so much pain that you will experience delirium while swimming,
you won't be able to climb out of the water unassisted, and
you will only be able to sleep for a maximum of five hours
each night.

## Sunburn, Death, and Other Dangers

Wear a wetsuit and use lots of Vaseline to reduce chafing. Dangers include sunburn (even if you wear plenty of sunblock, face mask, and a hat, your face will blister and your second-degree burns may become infected), heat exhaustion, dehydration, muscle cramps, abrasions, piranhas, crocodiles, bull sharks, larvae infections, and the infamous toothpick fish, which swims up your pee stream while you urinate and camps in your urethra.

Sometimes your support crew will need to tip buckets of animal blood into the water to distract predators. The current flows constantly; floating debris and unpredictable currents are serious threats. Towards the end of the swim as you near the sea, the ocean tides will push you upriver, so you'll have to use all your energy just to move forward. Allow yourself at least eight months to recover.

# 73. Have a Sex Change in Thailand:

There are two types of sex change surgery (SCS): chopping bits off and sewing bits on. Both require a lot of surgical skill, a clean-ish room, and a surgeon who doesn't ask too many questions—or even speak your language. Welcome to Bangkok, where SCS is so commonplace that it is advertised on the Internet and in the classified section of newspapers.

## Qualifications

To qualify for surgery, you must have already been living as a member of the opposite sex for a signifi-cant period of time (at least two years), and have two testimonials from mental health professionals stating that you would make a good candidate for SCS, and that you are mentally capable of making this decision. You should also have been on hormone therapy for a year. In Thailand, although there are guidelines, the doctors aren't obliged to demand any of the above, so you could walk in off the street in the morning, slap a roll of bills on the counter, and hobble out a different sex in the afternoon (although you'll have to stay in a nearby hotel for two weeks and come in every day to get your dressings changed).

## Menu

Genital reconstruction surgery in a good Thai clinic will cost you less than $15,000, a fraction of what surgeons charge in the United States (in sketchier clinics they'll chop it off for two grand). How can they do it so cheaply? Well for starters, they don't waste money on big plush offices. Everything takes place in a little room off a busy downtown street.

## The Procedure

Male-to-female surgery takes about four hours; female-to-male takes at least three separate surgeries because there's stuff to chop off plus reconstructive surgery. Possible complications include blood clots, leakages from the backside or bladder, and infections. You are advised to stop smoking a month before the surgery to improve your skin quality and healing rate, and to reduce the risk of blood clots. If you are going male-to-female, don't be ripped off by two water-filled condoms for breast implants.

## Medical Certificate

After the surgery, make sure you are issued a medical certificate stating that you have undergone sex reassignment surgery. When you get home, you will need it to legally change your name and amend your birth certificate, and to show to your parents.

# 74. Travel to the Future:

Time traveling into the future is easier than traveling into the past. Dystopian writers have predicted the horrors that await us there, but the future can't be that bad because it hasn't happened yet; paradoxically, this is precisely the reason why it's theoretically possible to go there.

## Models of Future Time Travel

There are two models of future time travel. In one model, you leave your present and travel to a future in which you are only present as the future traveler, since you have removed yourself from the present (and hence the future) at your moment of travel. In other words, if you had a driving test tomorrow and you wanted to see if you passed or failed, you would travel in time to tomorrow, where you would discover that you hadn't taken the test at all, since you had inexplicably gone missing.

In the second model, you are transported to your own personal future, where you may even meet your future self (so long as you don't travel beyond your own natural lifetime). You could even shake hands with yourself on your deathbed.

## Methods of Future Time Travel

Physics allows for future time travel without building a fictional "time machine." Simply travel away from the earth at close that the speed of light for a few years, then turn around and travel back home. Einstein showed that time is relative to the observer, so you will find that scores of years have passed on Earth and everyone you ever knew will be dead. Alternatively, take up temporary residence inside a hollow high-mass object, or just outside the event horizon of a black hole.

## Three Things That Shouldn't Happen in the Future

1. If life is a computer-generated illusion and human beings are nothing more than wet cells that generate electricity for their mechanical overlords, and you manage to stop four sentinels just by thinking it, don't let anyone reason that you could pull it off with a sloppy answer like: "Because you are the One."

2. If Kevin Costner's *Waterworld* is the reality and drinking-water has become one of the world's rarest commodities, explain to the raft-dwellers of the future that they can desalinate sea water by simply boiling it and then collecting the condensation.

3. If you've been to the year 3000, where not much has changed but they live underwater, you will NOT encounter the great-great-great-granddaughter of anyone from your own time—she would have died during the 23rd century.

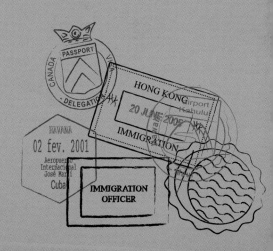

# 75. Drive Like a Maniac:

Driving's tough and it's getting tougher. All over the world the roads are full of idiots who are out to get you, and that's just the pedestrians. The lunatics in their cars are even worse; they'll slow you down, cut you off, they'll overtake you, and destroy your no claims bonus. But at last there's a way to fight back and show them who is boss. Get mad, get bad, and get even. In short: drive like an even bigger nut job than them.

## Getting a Grip

The steering wheel is one of the most important parts of the car. It is one of the things you hold when you are driving. It is the thing that puts YOU in control. Never use two hands—this is unsafe because it makes you tense up and become over cautious. The best holding posture is to rest your hand on your lap and hook your thumb around the bottom of the wheel (at 5 o'clock). This leaves your other hand free for cell phone maneuvers, picking your nose, holding a map, opening the glove compartment, eating, flipping the bird, playing cards, emptying the ashtray, and changing the tax disc. At all other times drive with your right arm behind the passenger seat.

## Road Rage

This is the body's natural response to other people's stupid and nonsensical driving. What can send a driver into a fit of road rage? Here are six typical reasons. How many have you experienced today?

1. The person in front is driving like a maniac.

2. You are now at least twenty minutes late.

3. You begin talking to yourself—common phrases include "He's done it again," "Come on!", "Jesus, did you see that!" "What's gone wrong with my life?" "I deserve better than this" "Where's my gun?"

4. The person in front has a better car than you.

5. You feel like a failure and can't understand why you're stuck behind an idiot, when Brad Pitt is having a fantastic life.

6. You married the wrong person.

To stop feeling road rage, first accept that when you drive you will inevitably encounter lots of stupid and mindless morons. Try to face your own sexual inadequacy. You are well on the way to eliminating yourself from the human gene pool.

## Road Kill

On a cold October evening, there's nothing better than to see a pair of eyes twinkling innocently in the darkness ahead. Turn up the radio and waste the sucker—unless you are driving in Sweden—in which case it may be a 600 lb brown elk. (Swerve for anything bigger than a opossum.) If you cannot find a moving target then it can be just as pleasurable to bump over an animal that is already dead. Rigor mortis sure does harden 'em up quick (see page 173 for cooking tips).

## Traffic Jams

In a traffic jam, it is your responsibility to keep the other passengers informed about your schedule. For example, if seventy-two miles of your journey remains and you have been traveling at an average speed of four miles per hour for the last half hour, you should announce that at this rate you won't reach your destination for another eighteen hours. Bang on the steering wheel for emphasis.

Always change into a faster lane. It is a myth created by police that all lanes in a traffic jam are traveling at the same speed.

## Accidents

The most important thing to remember after an accident is who gets the blame. After a collision, if you are conscious, immediately jump out of your car and launch into a stream of vulgar abuse, then phone your lawyer. Even if the accident was your fault, this will plant a seed of doubt in any reasonable person's mind.

# 76. Journey to the Most Dangerous Locations:

Some of the world's hazard hot spots didn't cut it, such as Burundi, Sri Lanka, and the Gaza Strip, but don't book your tickets just yet; for the purposes of this list, there can be only five. In no particular order, here they are:

## Afghanistan

While coalition forces continue to fight the Taliban, there is a high risk of kidnapping and assassination, especially outside the capital of Kabul. The place is still crawling with al-Qaida terrorists, and there are thousands of unexploded mines and artillery stashes.

## Iraq

Despite the coalition PR, nowhere in Iraq is safe to visit, including the supposedly safe Green Zone in Baghdad. People continue to be killed daily in insurgent attacks, and healthcare and other government infrastructure is completely screwed.

## Somalia

There is no American embassy, so if you get into trouble you're on your own. There are frequent attacks on foreigners, and inter-clan fighting means that the weak Transitional Federal Government controls only parts of the South.

## Democratic Republic of Congo

Even though the civil war is over, active rebel groups are a major threat, and tension and crime are still high. Carjackings, kidnappings, rape, and murder are commonplace, often at the hands of troops.

## Côte d'Ivoire

Following an uprising in 2002, a "government of national unity" was put in place, but the country remains very unstable. A peace deal between the government and the rebels was signed in 2007, but violent crime and armed robbery are still big threats.

# 77. Avoid Getting Knifed at a Truck Stop:

A trucker rest stop can be an intimidating place, full of clinically obese guys who have been on the road for fifteen hours straight and want nothing more than a caffeine-and-sugar rush, an all-you-can-eat buffet, and to kill a prostitute. It's not the best place to strike up a conversation, but if you're stuck for small talk and silence in the stalls makes you nervy, here's what NOT to say:

1. "Hi. My name's Nigel and I'll be your weenie washer for today."

2. "Didn't I see you on that *Jerry Springer* crossdresser special last week?"

3. "You can haul my load any time."

4. "I was admiring your junk back there; it's a beauty."

5. "Would you like to see a photo of me with a semi?"

6. "Have you just dropped off a big load?"

7. "Plaid really brings out the color of your eyes."

8. "You look like you're running low and hard."

9. "Did you know that each gallon of gasoline burned by your truck releases 24 lbs of $CO_2$ into the atmosphere?"

10. "Wow! I bet you won't be putting that one in your log book."

# 78. Climb the Pyramids:

The three great pyramids of Giza are located on the Giza Plateau a few miles southwest of Cairo, in Egypt. Climbing them is illegal, since it damages the stones and the 51 degree incline is very steep; many people have been killed in the attempt.

## An Irresistible Challenge

When the pyramids were built they were surfaced with highly polished white limestone casing stones to create a dazzling smooth surface. Over the centuries, most of these stones have been either eroded or stolen to expose the stair-like structure that now beckons us to climb.

## Bribe the Guards

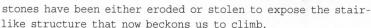

A daytime ascent is not suggested because you would simply be caught and arrested by the guards. You must sneak into the compound under the cover of darkness, at about 3 A.M.. Guards with dogs still patrol the perimeter of the complex, but if caught you may be able to bribe them.

Make your way to the north face of the pyramids, which are in relative darkness (the sides that face Cairo are illuminated with spotlights). Menkaure is the smallest and easiest pyramid to climb and it is also the furthest away from the entrance, but at 204 feet it is less than half the height of the others. You won't be able to reach the very top of the middle pyramid, Khafre, because it still has casing stones at the summit, but Khufu, the real challenge, is there for the taking.

## Pyramid of Khufu

Khufu is the oldest and tallest of the pyramids and the only surviving member of the Seven Wonders of the Ancient World. It was completed in 2560 B.C. and remained the tallest manmade structure in the world for more than 3,800 years (until the construction of the spire of Lincoln Cathedral in Great Britain in 1300 A.D.). It was 480 feet high, but with erosion it now stands 455 feet high. The record ascent and descent time was achieved by an Egyptian guide who could climb up and down in less than seven minutes. He used to perform this feat for visiting dignitaries at the command of President Nasser.

## Enjoy the View

When you reach the summit, you will enjoy a spectacular view of Cairo and the desert, and can ponder about the people who have stood at the same vantage point. In 1798, just before the Battle of Giza, Napoleon Bonaparte observed, "From atop these pyramids, forty centuries look down upon you." Soak it up—you will probably fall and break your neck during the treacherous descent.

# 79. Walk the Length of Great Britain Naked:

Land's End in Cornwall is the extreme southwestward tip of Great Britain, and John O'Groats, in Caithness, Scotland, is traditionally the most northern (although nearby Dunnet Head is actually farther north). The distance between these two points by road is 874 miles, and while plenty of people have walked this route, only one man, former Royal Marine Stephen Gough, has completed the journey on foot, stark naked—twice.

## Know Why You Are Doing It

Make sure you understand your reasons for making your journey in the buff. Speaking during his ordeal as he battled through the bitterly cold winds and driving rain of the Scottish Highlands, Gough mused: "When I first started doing this I thought I had reasons. I thought I knew why. But the more I go on I realize that there isn't a reason." You will be joined by lots of fellow naked walkers who want to support you; expect some press attention, especially when you are being arrested. You may even get beaten up (on his first attempt,

Gough was attacked by a group of teenagers at St. Ives). You'll need firm resolve to see it through.

## Legal Problems

The biggest challenge apart from the weather is that you will be repeatedly arrested for public indecency. Stephen Gough carried a backpack and wore nothing but a pair of socks and hiking boots, and occasionally a hat. Under ordinary circumstances, the journey could be completed comfortably within a few weeks, but it took him seven months because he was arrested fifteen times, and spent a total of 140 nights in prison, mainly due to his refusal to wear clothes in court.

On his second hike, Gough was accompanied by his naked girlfriend, Melanie Roberts; they were arrested in England, but released immediately. Like them, you will experience the most trouble in Scotland where the indecency laws are stricter. In your defence you may claim, like Gough, that Article 6 of the European Convention on Human Rights—Right to a Fair Trial—is being breached by making you wear clothes in court. But you'll still get beaten up.

# 80. Break Out of the Bangkok Hilton:

The Klong Prem prison in Thailand, better known as the Bangkok Hilton, houses around 12,000 prisoners, with about 600 being *farangs* (Westerners), doing hard time, or waiting for their drug smuggling cases to come to trial. Only one Westerner has ever escaped from the prison—David McMillan—whose recently-published book *Escape* describes his amazing feat. His philosophy is simple: "There are only three truly important things in successful escaping: the will to leave; the ability to keep secrets; and most importantly, having close friends."

## Breakout Advice

From the moment you arrive you must have the mindset of a survivor and escapee. Anyone smuggling more than 100 grams of drugs spends their prison sentence (or last few weeks before execution) chained. McMillan anticipated this by "losing" his charge sheet and showing the guards a lawyer's card on which he had previously scribbled "41.9 grams." He avoided being chained, which meant he could escape.

There will be about 700 people in your prison block. Most of them will raise the alarm if they

see you escaping, so you must avoid being seen by both prisoners and the guards manning the eighteen command towers dotted
around the complex. Escape is impossible without the coopera-
tion of your cellmates. McMillan shared a cell with four other
men, three of whom assisted, and the other one was intimidated
into keeping quiet.

Build up a network of friends and allies inside and outside
the prison. That way you can smuggle supplies into the prison
to aid your escape. Currency within the prison is money and
sachets of aspirin called *Tam Jai* ("strong heart"). Steal the
rest of the items from prison workshops.

Here are some items that you will need to escape: 160 feet
of army boot webbing, four hacksaw blades, oil, clean pants
for outside (prisoners wear shorts), four rolls of gaffer
tape, eight picture frames, bamboo poles, heavy rubber
gloves, bottled drinking water, collapsible umbrella,
and backup passport.

## The Plan

1. **Begin at midnight. Use the hacksaw blades to saw
through a one-inch thick bar in your cell window. This
will take about two and a half hours. Cut through the
bottom of the bar, and two-thirds of the way through the
top, and then bend to make a gap. Wrap wet towels on the
bars as you saw to reduce vibrations and muffle the noise.**

2. **Wedge a plank through the bottom of the bar. Take off
your shirt and oil your upper body. Give money to your
cellmates so that in the morning they can bribe the guards
to reduce their punishment for not notifying them about
your escape.**

3. Squeeze through the eight-inch gap, tie the webbing to the plank, and rappel to the floor fifty feet below.

4. Break into a nearby prison workshop (preferably the paper box factory). Select eight bamboo poles, and strap them to the picture frames using the gaffer tape to make two ladders. Scale three major and two minor walls. This will take you the rest of the night. Before you reach the final outer wall, use your ladders to bridge "Mars Bar Creek," an eight-foot-wide trench steaming with raw sewage.

5. Wash with the remainder of the bottled water, change your clothes, and put on the rubber gloves before climbing the prison's electric fence. By now it will be about 6:00 A.M. and daybreak.

6. Skirt the outside of the prison under the cover of your black collapsible umbrella and walk calmly to the main road where you can hail a taxi. No one will suspect you're an escapee because prisoners don't carry umbrellas.

7. Get to the airport as quickly as possible, stopping only at a friend's house to collect false documents to get you out of the country.

# 81. Become a Cliff-Diving Thrill Seeker:

Cliff diving or "tombstoning" leaves little room for error. When you jump from a height of eighty feet, your body is subjected to ten Gs and the impact as you hit the water is the equivalent of slamming into concrete from a height of twenty feet, so your entry has to be correct or you're in serious trouble.

Here are the top ten places to get your cliff diving on:

### 1. Kahekili's Leap, Lanai, Hawaii

This is the birthplace of cliff diving. Kahekili was an eighteenth-century king who instructed his Nakoa warriors to display their bravery and loyalty by freefalling seventy feet over jagged rocks into the clear blue ocean below. The practice was called *lele kawa*.

### 2. Wolfgangsee, Austria

Each summer the cliffs at Hochzeitskreuz, Wolfgangsee play host to the Red Bull Cliff Diving World Championships where the fourteen best cliff divers in the world jump from a height of eighty-eight feet in front of three thousand fans. They somersault and twist in the air for 2.5 seconds before hitting the water at fifty-five miles per hour.

### 3. La Quebrada, Acapulco, Mexico

The spot's name means "The Break" in Spanish, and this is one of the top tourist attractions in Mexico. The cliff jump is sixty feet high. Divers must time their jump precisely because the water level changes as the waves roll in and out of the cove. Formed in 1934, La Quebrada Cliff Divers still perform death-defying cliff jumps nightly while holding torches.

### 4. Ponte Brolla, Vallemaggia, Switzerland

The World High Diving Federation Cliff Diving European Championships is held here regularly, but there is a range of diving heights from junior (thirty feet) to more challenging (sixty-five feet). If splitting your head or feet open on impact isn't painful enough, the icy water will probably give you a heart attack.

### 5. Porto Venere, Italy

Porto Venere is a beautiful medieval town on the Ligurian coast of Italy, south of the Cinque Terre known worldwide for its natural beauty. There are lots of cliff-diving venues on this coast, but this is one of the best.

### 6. Red Rocks Park, South Burlington, Vermont

Vermont is loaded with good cliff diving, but Red Rocks Park offers drops of up to seventy-six feet, with narrow rock walls to increase the chances of fatal injury. Jumping into the icy waters here requires even greater precision than other dive sites.

### 7. Tar Creek Falls, California

This seventy-foot-high double waterfall in Los Padres
National Forest is very challenging. If you push out too far,
you hit massive purple boulders beneath; too little and you
hit the falls. The water is icy cold and the climb to the top
is lengthy and demanding.

### 8. Cedar Creek Falls, San Diego, California

The ninety-minute hike from the parking lot to these spectacular falls is well worth it. Four miles away from the Falls
is the Devil's Punch Bowl, another popular jump site. Spring
is the best time to jump; otherwise water levels are too low.

### 9. Rick's Café, Negril, Jamaica

Tourists have been breaking their spines and sternums here
since Negril's premier haunt opened in the early '70s. The
thirty-five-foot cliff jump looks safe, but even from that
height you can really mess yourself up. If so, the "lifeguards"
will strap you to a piece of wooden fence and drag you back up
the cliffs to receive "expert" medical attention.

### 10. Hoover Dam, Nevada-Arizona Border

When you jump the Hoover Dam you die. This is the ulti-
mate tomb-stone challenge—a 726 foot drop into the Colorado
River. There is no fence or barrier so certain death is just a
30-inch concrete ledge away.

# 82. Annoy Your Fellow Airline Passengers:

If you really want to get on people's nerves in the air, it's no use monopolizing the arm rests, or kicking the seat in front of you for hours. Those annoyances have all been tried before, so let your imagination run free. Here are ten suggestions to get you started:

1. Smuggle fifty pairs of nail clippers on board and then start handing them out for free just before take off. This should ground the plane for several hours.

2. Boast to everyone how you've got the safest seat on the plane. Make those who are sitting in the most dangerous seats aware of their bad planning and back up your argument with lots of statistics.

3. Be a two-year-old.

4. Call the flight attendant "nurse" and boast loudly that you have converted your nipples into smoke detectors.

5. Claim that Capt. Chesley Sullenberger III is your fifth cousin six times removed, and then draw an elaborate family tree showing the connection.

6. Fly Saudi Airlines then refuse to allow the plane to take off until all foreign-looking people with moustaches have been removed.

7. Spend the whole flight counting out loud how many times the person next to you blinks, and challenge them to a staring competition.

8. Scribble the names of people you would like to kill on your carry-on, and your forehead.

9. Make a life-sized origami model of Charles Lindbergh out of sick bags.

10. Play with your beard nervously, fiddle with your shoe, spend a few minutes praying, then fire up your laptop and hit this link: *http://boortz.com/mp3/archive/countdown.swf*

# 83. Combat Culture Shock:

Culture shock occurs when a traveler in a foreign country is cut off from the familiar cultural reference points of home and is exposed to so many alien experiences—strange sounds, sights, smells, customs, toilets—that they suffer physiological and psychological stress. The key to combating culture shock is to recognize the symptoms quickly and to adopt the coping mechanisms of the seasoned expat.

## Symptoms

Symptoms typically appear about a month after arrival, when the novelty of being abroad is replaced by feelings of rootlessness, homesickness, irritation, frustration, loneliness, and a general feeling of apathy and hunger. If you experience any of these signs, seek out your expat community. If symptoms persist past six months, see a doctor (not there—when you get home).

## Coping Mechanisms

1. Recognize that the problem is with them, not with you. Observe how others are acting in the same situation and resolve that you won't lose your cultural identity and go native.

2. Don't view things as right or wrong. It's just wrong, that's all.

3. Don't learn their language—otherwise they will think you are stupid (consider how stupid foreigners sound when they try to speak your language). All you need to know is to count from one to ten, how to hail a taxi, and demand a room without cockroaches. If you can't make yourself understood, don't internalize your frustration and anger.

4. Accept that your culture is superior to theirs, but don't lord it over them. It's not their fault that their government is corrupt and the per capita GDP is less than the price of a cup of coffee back home.

5. Laugh it off: developing cultural stereotypes about the new way of life helps you and your fellow expats to blow off some steam.

# 84. Access the Disney Tunnels:

As legend has it, Walt Disney was walking around Disneyland when he saw a Frontierland cowboy walking through Fantasyland. He thought it looked wrong and destroyed the magic, so he tasked the Imagineers building Disney World at the time with designing a system of utility corridors ("Utilidors") underneath the Magic Kingdom to allow employees and supplies to move around unseen. They can only be accessed by "Cast Members" (employees) with special ID cards.

## Tunnel Construction

Since Florida is a giant swamp, the tunnels aren't really underground at all. When Walt Disney World was built, the tunnels (which are about fifteen feet high) were constructed on ground level. Using the earth that was dug out to make the Seven Seas Lagoon, the tunnels were buried and the park was built on the second story.

## Layout

The layout of the tunnels is straightforward. There is a rough octagonal outer tunnel bisected by a tunnel running from the security offices at the front of Main Street to Cinderella's Castle in Fantasyland; plus there are several short offshoots. Unmarked access doors are dotted around the Magic Kingdom.

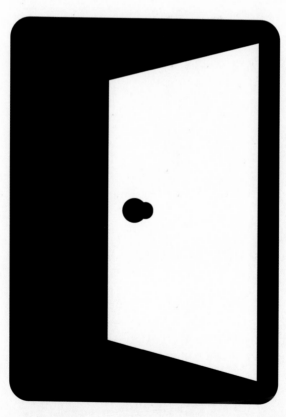

Behind each door is a flight of stairs which takes you down into the operational hub, where there are rehearsal facilities, offices, a cafeteria, changing rooms, and the digital control center which controls all the rides and parades. All the trash is sucked down here by an automated vacuum system to a central refuse area. On the floor of the tunnels are color-coded lines directing you from land to land. This buried city covers an area of 392,000 square feet.

## How to Hack into the Utilidors

First you need to steal an ID card from one of the Cast Members. The best place to pickpocket victims is in the employees' parking lot about a mile from the main tunnel entrance, where cast members show their security pass, to get on a bus, which takes them into the tunnels. Once you've stolen a pass you'll need to use it quickly before it is reported missing and access privileges are cancelled. Alternatively, you could steal an ID from a cast member inside the Magic Kingdom. Walk up to Donald Duck and as him to pose for a photo. Give him a big hug and while your friend composes the shot, locate the Velcro fastenings in his costume, stick your hand into his pocket and steal Donald's ID. Then use the map to locate the access points, or follow other characters to see where they go.

# 85. Find the Ark of the Covenant:

The Ark of the Covenant is the wooden box that housed Aaron's rod, some *manna* (the miracle food which kept the Israelites alive before matza balls were invented), and the sacred Tablets of Stone which Moses brought down from Mount Sinai, bearing the Ten Commandments.

## Magic Box

The Ark was a powerful talisman for the Israelites, who carried it around with them in the wilderness, and into battle, born by Levite priests, 2,000 cubits (about half a mile) in front of them. Its magical powers helped to part the Red Sea, and it was carried round the Walls of Jericho seven times before they eventually crumbled at the sound of rams' horns. Whenever it was carried, it was always wrapped in tachash skins and a blue cloth.

## Where Did You Last See It?

As your mother will tell you, the best way to find something is to work out when it was last seen, which in the case of the Ark, was 2,500 years ago. We know that it was housed in the First Temple by Solomon around 950 B.C. Later it is mentioned in the Old Testament in II Chronicles 35:3, when King Josiah (who ruled in the seventh century B.C.) instructed the Levites: "Put the holy ark in the house which Solomon the son of David, king of Israel, built; you need no longer carry it upon your shoulders." Scholars don't know whether the Levites followed his instructions, although if they'd been carrying it around for 350 years, they must have been glad to rest.

## Possible Hiding Places

1. Nebuchadnezzar destroyed the Temple in 586 B.C., so if the Ark was there it could also have been destroyed or taken to Babylon (although it isn't mentioned in the book of Jeremiah with all the other spoil). Babylon is in present-day Iraq about fifty-five miles south of Baghdad. Good luck with that one.

2. Jeremiah hid it on Mount Nebo shortly before the Babylonian attack, or possibly one of the many caves in the area where the Dead Sea Scrolls were found.

3. According to biblical scholar Leen Ritmeyer, there's a rectangular hollow carved out in the bedrock of the Muslim Dome of the Rock Shrine in Jerusalem, with exactly the same dimensions as the Ark. He believes this is the site of the Second Temple. The hollow is empty, which indicates that the Ark could well be in Ritmeyer's garage. However, there is also a complex system of secret chambers underneath the Shrine, but the Supreme Muslim Council, the Wakf, hasn't allowed any excavations on the site and many scholars believe that the Ark was never placed in the Second Temple at all.

4. Another candidate is the Church of St. Mary of Zion in Axum, Ethiopia. The Ethiopian Orthodox Church claims to have possessed the Ark, of the Covenant since the early Middle Ages. It is guarded by a large group of bouncer monks with instructions to kill all intruders who attempt to enter the Holy of Holies where the Ark is kept. Only one monk is allowed access to the Ark, and, once appointed, he spends the rest of his life in the Holy of Holies— never to be allowed out again. Apply for the position in writing, enclosing a stamped addressed envelope with your application.

Church of St. Mary of Zion in Axum

# 86. Visit Sodom and Gomorrah:

The cities of Sodom and Gomorrah are remembered today as the epitome of decadence; according to the Bible, they were destroyed by fire and brimstone falling from the sky, and Lot's wife was famously turned into a pillar of salt when she turned back to look at the destruction.

## Cities of the Plain

Sodom and Gomorrah were two of five cities known as the Cities of the Plain, along with Zoar, Admah, and Zeboim. Archaeologists have located the actual site of these cities, although the night life isn't what it used to be.

For many years it was believed that the cities were fictional, mainly because scholars didn't think there was a route east of the River Jordan as described in the Bible. Then they discovered that eastern travel was possible, and expeditions set out to locate the remains.

In 1924, pioneering biblical archaeologist William F. Allbright conducted a search south of the Dead Sea, and just above the plain he found the ruins of a large fortress. He didn't realize then that he had discovered Sodom. During the 1960s and 1970s, the search was extended to include the east side of the Dead Sea, and the other four Cities of the Plain were located, dating back between four and five thousand years. Ash and charcoal deposits suggested these sites had been destroyed by fire.

## Fire and Brimstone

The destruction of the cities is described in Genesis 19:23–25: "Then the Lord rained upon Sodom and upon Gomorrah brimstone and fire from the Lord out of heaven; And he over-threw those cities, and all the plain, and all the inhabitants of the cities, and that which grew upon the ground." The area beneath the plain contains rich deposits of petroleum, natural gas, bitumen, and sulphur, so it is likely that an earthquake could have brought these chemicals shooting to the surface, where they would have ignited causing the cataclysm described in the Bible. The Bible also describes what Abraham saw. He was to the west of the Dead Sea, and from his vantage point saw "dense smoke rising from the land, like smoke from a furnace," which is further evidence of a petroleum fire.

## That's Your Lot

After you've soaked up the atmosphere on the Plains, pay a visit to Mount Sodom along the southwestern part of the Dead Sea in Israel, which is made entirely of rock salt. This is the only place in the world where you can climb rocks 1,200 feet and still be below sea level. One of the halite pillars at its summit is all that remains of Lot's wife.

# 87. Break into the Bedroom of Queen Elizabeth II:

On July 9, 1982, an unemployed father of four, Michael Fagan, broke into Buckingham Palace and reached the Queen's bedroom, whereupon he sat on the edge of her bed and chatted with her for half an hour. The only other person to have achieved this incredible feat is Homer Simpson.

The Metropolitan Police are responsible for security of royal sites; they provide the Royal Protection Squad—the Royal Family's bodyguards. If you want to try your luck, here is your five-step guide to crashing the Queen's pad.

1. Scaling the walls and fences is easy. On his first attempt (he successfully broke in twice), Fagin shimmied up a drainpipe onto the roof and then climbed through an unlocked window on the

POLICE NATIONALE
Aéroport de Paris
26 NOV. 1998
FRANCE

roof. In 1991, another man got within yards of the Queen's private apartments, and the following year Kevin McMahon was arrested inside the palace grounds twice in one week. In 1997, an escaped mental patient was caught wandering around the grounds; in September 2003, a Fathers 4 Justice campaigner dressed as Batman climbed on to a ledge as part of a protest over a court case.

2. Dress code is very informal. Leave your bowtie at home; in fact, leave your shoes there too. Fagin just wore pants and a white T-shirt, and was barefoot. In 1994, an American paraglider, James "Fanman" Miller, landed on the palace roof naked.

3. Once inside, go straight to the Queen's bedroom. The best time to enter is just before the security officer guarding her room goes off duty. He will walk the Queen's dogs before changing shift, leaving the door unguarded for a few minutes.

4. Knock on the door before entering. This is the Queen of England, so show a little respect. Sit on the edge of her bed and talk to her about horses.

5. Bring your own cigarettes. The only reason Fagan was caught was because he tried to mooch a cigarette from the monarch; she picked up the phone and called security. They came, eventually.

# 88. Hunt a Yeti in the Himalayas:

The Himalayas are the highest range of mountains in the world. The "roof of the world" is home to Mount Everest, and the yeti, which most people agree is a giant hairy bipedal ape. The Nepalese call it *Ban-manche* (forest man) and *Kangchenjunga rachyyas* (Kangchenjunga's demon). If you want to find the yeti, wrap up warm and start climbing.

## Dhaulagiri

The hottest recent yeti sightings have been on the slopes of Dhaulagiri, the world's fifth highest mountain, in western Nepal. Japan's most famous yeti-hunter, Yoshiteru Takahashi claims to have found a yeti cave here, but his camera froze before he could take a picture. However, on subsequent expeditions to the area, he has photographed footprints using nine motion-sensitive cameras.

## Friend or Foe

In most encounters the yeti has run away, so it would probably flee, unless it was cornered, or very hungry. Run-ins
with the yeti have been both hostile and friendly. A Sherpa
girl was dragged off by the yeti, who released her after she
screamed, and then killed two of her yaks; by contrast, in
1938, Captain d'Auvergue, the curator of the Victoria Memorial
in Calcutta, India, reported that he was cared for by a nine-
foot-tall yeti after becoming snowblind.

## Ape with Altitude

Most sightings of the yeti have occurred at altitudes
between 15,000 and 20,000 feet. Sightings have been reported
since the early nineteenth century, but the first reliable one
took place in 1925. Greek photographer N. A. Tombazi spotted
one about three hundred yards away at an altitude of 15,000
feet. He described a "figure in outline . . . exactly like a
human being" that "showed up dark against the snow." The creature disappeared, but Tombazi discovered fifteen footprints in
the snow measuring seven inches by four, with five toes.

In 1951, footprints eighteen inches long and thirteen inches
wide were photographed on the southwestern slopes of the Men-
lung Glacier, between Tibet and Nepal at an altitude of 20,000
feet. Your best chances of a sighting are at these high altitudes, where the landscape is most remote and undisturbed by
people. Avoid Everest, as there are too many lunatics trying
to kill themselves there and that will scare the yeti away.
As put by Edmund Hillary, the first man to conquer Everest:
"There is precious little in civilization to appeal to a yeti."

# 89. Be a World-Class Hobo:

The definition of a hobo is someone who wanders around, without a permanent home or job. Hobo, bum, deadbeat—the terms are not interchangeable. A hobo is a cut above the other two because he is prepared to work to support his nomad lifestyle, rather than lie on a park bench drinking.

Unless you have a large sum of money sitting in the bank, you will have to be resourceful and use your skills to the fullest to get work on on the spot that can give you a reasonable standard of living, without being tied to one place. The standard of living you are prepared to tolerate is up to you, but if you want a warm place to sleep and decent food without resorting to begging, you'll need to do some planning. Yep, in today's harsh world, even being a hobo requires a little forward scheduling.

## Examine Your Skill Base

Hobos have traditionally been associated with manual labor, but you don't have to restrict yourself to odd jobs, fruit picking, dog walking, cooking, or farm work. Have you considered a hobo career in writing or running a successful website? Both these jobs leave you free to travel the world. Other nice gigs if you can get them are house-sitting, being a property caretaker, or basically any job where you can get rent-free living in exchange for services rendered. Think about your needs and the most efficient way to meet them.

## Give and Take

Don't be afraid to rely on friends—sacking out on someone's floor for a few nights is fine, so long as you don't overstay your welcome. Make a list of your connections and pay them a quick visit. Most of them will be pleased to see you and you can rely on their hospitality. Offer to do some odd jobs for them to repay their kindness.

Join a social networking group like the Freemasons or Rotary International—you can turn up at one of their meetings anywhere in the world and you'll usually be welcomed, and be offered a place to spend the night and a home-cooked meal.

## Transportation

You don't have to walk or ride the train. A cheap car can be a hobo's best friend—you can sleep in it when you can't afford a roof over your head, and you can drive around to find work. Gas and maintenance can be a drain on your resources, but a car gives you the freedom to roam. A motorcycle is cheaper, but you can't sleep or get laid in it.

## Follow the Hobo Code

As inscribed in the Annual Convention Congress of the Hobos of America held on August 8, 1894 at the Hotel Alden in Chicago, Illinois:

1. Decide your own life, don't let another person run or rule you.

2. When in town, always respect the local law and officials, and try to be a gentleman at all times.

3. Don't take advantage of someone who is in a vulnerable situation, the locals' or other hobos.

4. Always try to find work, even if temporary, and always seek out jobs nobody wants. By doing so you not only help a business along, but insure employment should you return to that town again.

5. Do not allow yourself to become a stupid drunk and set a bad example for the "locals'" treatment of other hobos.

6. When hanging out in town, respect handouts, do not wear them out; another hobo will be coming along who will need them as bad, if not worse than you.

7. Always respect nature; do not leave garbage.

8. If there's a community garden, always pitch in and help.

9. Try to stay clean, and wash up wherever possible.

10. Help your fellow hobos whenever and wherever needed—you may need their help someday.

# 90. Take a Road Trip in Style:

Unless you become a fugitive, you'll probably only make one major road trip in your life, so you may as well do it in style. Just because you can't afford an RV (which only does eight miles to the gallon) doesn't mean you have to settle for a rusty old heap that needs constant work just to keep you moving. Spend a little at the outset and gain a whole lot more down the line.

## Jacked-Up Suspension

The bigger the lift, the bigger your wheels can be; the two most popular kits are suspension lifts and body lifts. The standard suspension lifts will give you an extra 3", 6", or 8" to improve off-road performance, but since you are going to be parking in plenty of scenic spots like Glacier Point in Yosemite, it's more the look you're after. Body lifts, use blocks instead of springs to raise the body and are cheaper than suspension lifts but standard kits will only raise you 1" to 3".

## Window Tint

Nothing says purveyor of illegal narcotics more succinctly than dark windows. They're dope plus they protect you from the sun's damaging UV rays, heat, and glare (but not bullets) as you sit and watch the shrimp boats pull into a sleepy dock somewhere along the Atlantic coast route.

## Super Shiny Rims and Phat Tires

If you ain't got these, you ain't road-tripping. We recommend chrome spinning rims that spin even while you car is standing still. If you want performance (speed and fuel economy), choose light aluminum alloys over heavier chrome or steel. Always install rims that are at least 2" wider than the factory ones, as bigger wheels look radical. Check that the offset and the maximum-load rating suit your vehicle. Low profile tires look great with big rims and improve the handling, but they wear out quickly, give you a bumpier ride, suck in the snow, and they are very pricey—but you'll really stand out as the kind of Devil-may-care tripper who really knows how splash the cash.

## Under-Car Neons

Installing under-car neons is still the cheapest way to get you pulled over by the cops every time you hit the Appalachian Trail. Install a rocker switch so when necessary you can switch your illegal red-and-blue strobe configuration to something more hiker-friendly.

## Dope System

If God had meant us to drive along the Pacific Coast without bleeding ears, cars wouldn't have trunks. Fill yours up with as many woofers and sub woofers as you can fit in and turn up the volume until every bolt on the chassis has worked itself loose.

# 91. Roll Cheese at Cooper's Hill:

Once a year for the last two hundred years, the Cheese Rolling Festival has taken place at Cooper's Hill near Brockworth, four miles southeast of the city of Gloucester, in the United Kingdom. It is currently held on the country's Spring Bank Holiday Monday. You don't need to fill in any forms to enter; just turn up early at the top of the hill and chase the cheese in front of several thousand spectators.

## The Rules

The run is about 300 feet long and in places the incline is extremely steep. There are five official races, at twenty minute intervals, and then several unofficial "fun runs." There are also several up-hill races, which are less dangerous. On average, the St John's Ambulance treats between twenty to thirty injuries and there are four or five hospitalizations each year for broken ankles, cuts and bruises, and concussions.

The first race starts at midday. Contestants gather at the top of the hill; a round Double Gloucester cheese decorated with a blue and red ribbon is rolled, and the contestants have to chase it down the hill. The cheese is estimated to reach seventy miles per hour, and takes about twelve seconds to reach the bottom. The person who reaches the finish line first wins the cheese, and there are second- and third-place prizes as well.

## Race Tactics

Jason Crowther, from west Wales, has won the race three times, and when interviewed by the BBC in 2007 had this to say: "There's no training you can do for this. It was a bit slippery and I heard something crack, which I think was my knee. But there aren't any tactics involved, as you can probably see."

If you try to run down staying on your feet, you will pick up so much speed that you'll end up tumbling head over heels. This will actually increase your speed and may win you the race. If you fall, try to get back on your feet again as you are moving, then you can give it another burst of speed. If you want to avoid injury, shimmy and bounce down on your backside. However, losing control and tumbling head over heels usually covers the ground more quickly and most winners have done this at some point during the race. If the conditions are muddy, you can usually slide the last ten yards over the finish line, where "catchers" tackle you to kill your speed.

# 92. Claim Political Asylum:

If you don't want your vacation to end and you can't face your responsibilities back home, claiming asylum is a great way to stay at the party. The United Nations 1951 Convention Relating to the Status of Refugees and the 1967 Protocol Relating to the Status of Refugees provides the legislation that applies to asylum.

In order to claim asylum successfully, you must prove that you are unable to return to your home country, or your main country of residence if you are stateless because you fear persecution there under protected grounds, which include race, nationality, politics, religion, sexuality, and membership and/or participation in any particular social group or social activities.

## United Kingdom

The UK has a soft spot for asylum seekers, and receives the largest number of applications. This means that there's a huge backlog in processing, so even if your request is unsuccessful, in the meantime you'll be able to spend so many years in the country that you will be able to claim de facto citizenship and squatter's rights when the Queen tries to throw you out. You'll receive an allowance of about £40 a week, most of which is Fortnum & Mason food vouchers. After six months you can apply for the right to work, and you'll be given accommodation if you can prove you're destitute. Pray you get a hostel rather than a detention center.

**Pros:** the UK has the best justice system in the world, despite the Guildford Four, the Birmingham Six, the Bridgwater Four, and the M25 Three.

**Cons:** the beer is warm, but Brits don't care because they spend most of the time dumping it on their heads, and they can't watch a soccer match without throwing seats.

## Germany

Recently knocked off the top asylum spot by the UK, the pocket money isn't great (about 50 euro per week), you'll be housed in a reception center, and you won't have the right to work until your applications has been processed.

**Pros:** they are just like most of the folks back home: loud, fat, and carnivorous, except that they can speak better English.

**Cons:** their male tennis players have transparent eyebrows, all the stores close for lunch, and it takes seven minutes to pour a half pint of beer.

## France

There's a six-month waiting list for housing in an overcrowded reception center, and you need to apply for a temporary residence permit from the local authorities, for which there is also a six-month wait. Your allowance is four pounds of Camembert and two bottles of Vin de Table per day.

**Pros:** they have the most corrupt Olympic ice-skating judges in the world, and French women braid their underarm hair.

**Cons:** they think Jerry Lewis is a comic genius, per capita they buy the least soap and toothbrushes of any European country, and drugs are so prevalent in national sports that it is not uncommon for cyclists' heads to explode during the Alpine stages of the Tour de France.

# 93. Hack Your Cell Phone for Free Calls Abroad:

Calling friends in other countries can be very expensive, but you don't have to pay a penny if you use this simple hack. You don't need to buy a special phone, or download any software. Jaxtr allows you to use your cell phone to make calls in over fifty countries using Jaxtr's local numbers. Just follow these steps:

1. Go to: *www.jaxtr.com/user/index.jsp*

2. In the first box, enter your cell number, country, and country code.

3. In the second box, enter the mobile number, country, and country code of the person you want to call—let's call him Richard.

4. Click the orange button: "Get Jaxtr number."

5. On the next screen, enter your name and email address.

6. Jaxtr then gives you a local Jaxtr number for you to use every time you want to call Richard.

7. Dial the number. Jaxtr puts you on hold while it tries to connect you. It does this by sending Richard a text message telling him that you are trying to call. This message contains another number for Richard to call. Once he calls this number, Jaxtr connects you and you can talk for FREE.

# 94. Travel to Volatile Countries:

Back by popular demand, here are another five dangerous destinations that you'd be an idiot to head to. There still isn't room for Burundi, Sri Lanka, and the Gaza Strip, but in no particular order, avoid these first:

## Pakistan

Here, westerners are the target of suicide bombings from extremist Islamic groups, which have spread beyond their tribal bases and are trying to take over the entire nuclear-armed nation. The tribal areas bordering Afghanistan are especially volatile.

## Haiti

Violence and political instability are the norm; police corruption is widespread and the country has descended into lawlessness. Outside of the tourist resorts, visitors are at great risk of being robbed, raped, kidnapped, or murdered.

# Liberia

In 2003 the civil war ended, but the fragile peace is still being policed by a U.N. peacekeeping force, and crime is a major threat, including theft, rape, and murder.

# Chad

The country is very unstable with much fighting between various ethnic groups, especially at the border with the Darfur region of Sudan. Many westerners have been robbed at checkpoints and on the roads.

# Sudan

The United States has listed Sudan as a state sponsor of terrorism since 1993. The western region of Darfur is the most dangerous area of the country, as government-backed Janjaweed militias continue to terrorize locals in the name of suppressing anti-government rebels.

# 95. Look Tough in a Scary Neighborhood:

Sometimes there's just no avoiding a scary neighborhood, especially if you've booked a hostel on the wrong side of town, or you've got to go back to the 'hood to visit your parents.

1. Your clothing can send out "mug me" signals. Clearly, if you are wearing an expensive suit, carrying a Louis Vuitton bag, and making no attempt to hide the Rolex

Oyster on your wrist, then you can expect to attract trouble. However, even changing aspects of your appearance can make a big difference. If you wear a tie, take it off—it makes you look older, and more of a dork, and less likely to be able to handle yourself in a fight. Turn up the collar of your jacket as well—it gives you some edge.

2. Take your hands out of your pockets and walk purposefully and upright, with your shoulders back and your chest puffed out. Walking

around with hunched shoulders trying to make yourself look as small as possible doesn't make you any less conspicuous; it makes you look like a weak and easier target.

3. If you are wearing casual clothes, like a hoodie, wear the hood over your head to hide part of your face. If people can't see your face, they are less likely to challenge you.

4. Look every passer-by in the eye. Clearly, you don't want to hold the stare because this is confrontational, but only the weak stare at the floor and try to avoid the gaze of others.

5. Does talking to yourself mean you're crazy? Who knows, but most muggers won't want to take the risk, especially if there are plenty of silent targets around. The best type of crazy talk is muttering a stream of consciousness under your breath, and then shouting out a random word every twenty paces. This avoids looking like you're simply talking to your boss on your top-of-the-line Bluetooth earpiece and cell phone.

6. If you are confronted, speak loudly but slowly, and stay calm. Don't show any fear, and maintain eye contact. Explain that you won't cause any harm if they let you mind your own business. If they persist in harassing you, explain that you just got out of prison and you don't want another death on your conscience.

7. If none of this works, and they invade your personal space, hit them hard and fast; otherwise they will hit you first. Empty a can of pepper spray in their face, and then run like hell.

POLICE NATIONALE
Aéroport de Paris
26 NOV. 1998
FRANCE

# 96. Walk Along El Caminito del Rey:

*El Caminito del Rey* ("The King's little pathway") is a *via ferrata* (walkway) which runs along the walls of a narrow gorge in El Chorro, near Málaga, Spain. It was built over a hundred years ago, but this windswept trail where beauty meets danger is so unsafe that the local government has closed off the entrances (but a little metal fence and a warning sign in Spanish won't stop you, right?).

## The Construction

Construction began on the walkway in 1901 in order to link Chorro Falls with Gaitanejo Falls, so that supplies could be moved and workers on the hydroelectric power plants could gain access. It took four years to build, and it got its name in 1921 when King Alfonso XIII crossed the walkway for the state opening of the Conde del Guadalhorce Dam, in the days when it was relatively safe.

## Irresistible Challenge

The path varies between two and three feet in width, and it is nearly a thousand feet above the river. It is supported by steel beams attached to the rock face, but in many places the rusty metal is all that remains; most of the time there is no handrail.

In two separate incidents in 1999 and 2000, four people fell to their deaths prompting the closure of the path, but it is still an irresistible challenge for young backpackers and it has even inspired an Internet Flash game (see *www.abc.net.au/gameon/chasm/chasmgame.htm*).

Also check out this gnarly head-cam video taken by a hiker making the crossing: *http://jomzo.com/media/189/Scary_hiking_trail/*.

## Thrill Seekers in the Myst

There's something about the combination of rusty metal and old crumbling concrete that makes the pathway derelict-spooky as well as dangerous. There are several places where you can stare through holes in the crumbling concrete to the gorge floor below, others where there's no concrete at all for several feet. Crossing the bridge over the gorge, you'll enjoy the brief luxury of handrails on both sides, and you'll feel at your safest. Beyond there, the landscape simply becomes surreal—it feels like you've been transported back to 1993 and you are trapped in *Myst*. The final few feet are the worst, as the path narrows to a few inches and there is no handrail or wall. Stumble here and you will die.

In 2008, the President of Malaga Provincial Government, Salvador Pendon, announced plans for the restoration of El Caminito del Rey, so get down there soon before it becomes just another harmless tourist trap.

# 97. Climb Mount Everest without Oxygen:

At an altitude of 29,029 feet, the summit of the world's tallest mountain is near the physiological limit of what humans can endure. When Sir Edmund Hillary and Tensing Norgay climbed Everest in 1953, they used oxygen; it wasn't until 1978 that Reinhold Messner and Peter Habeler proved that it was possible to reach the summit without it. Since then a handful of people such as Messner and Ed Viesturs have reached the summit solo without oxygen.

## Health Risks

When you are at a high altitude, you are at risk from HACE (High Altitude Cerebral Edema—fluid on the brain). There is increased blood flow and fluid retention in the brain, which some climbers can tolerate better than others. Reinhold and Habeler drank lots of fluids during their ascent in 1978, but now it is thought that being a bit dehydrated is preferable because a dehydrated brain swells less. If you have a large skull and a small brain, you may also be at an advantage, but that probably applies to the majority of mountain climbers.

Within hours of being exposed to high altitude your breathing will increase, and there are changes in blood flow to the brain. You may assume you are thinking normally, but you'll have to keep testing yourself to check you aren't becoming hypoxic and irrational. The higher you go, the harder everything becomes. Prepare by spending long periods of time at higher-than-normal altitude to acclimatize. The expedition will take seven weeks, but only three of those will be spent climbing—the remainder will be resting and acclimatization. Signs of altitude sickness include headache, fainting and weakness, nausea, confusion, and death.

Other health risks, apart from falling off, include HAPE (High Altitude Pulmonary Edema, or fluid on the lungs)—listen for a death rattle at the end of each breath as a sign that you are drowning—as well as frostbite, hypothermia, sunburn, thrombosis, and trench foot. The dry air can also give you a hacking cough.

## Preparation

For a year before the climb increase your cardiovascular training by running eight miles each day on hilly terrain, four days on, one day off. Follow a weight training program to increase your upper body strength, and do lots of mountain climbing and hill walking. Gain an extra ten pounds in weight, as you will burn 6,000 calories a day on Everest and lose about 20 percent of your body weight.

The expedition will cost you about $50,000, minus what you save on seven canisters of oxygen.

# The Summit Attempt

At final camp, wake up at 9 P.M. and prepare to leave by
11 P.M., so that when you are half way to the summit the sun
will be rising (it's much easier to ascend in the dark than
descend). You should reach the summit by 11 A.M. the following
morning, having spent the last two hours climbing the final
300 feet, where energy requirements increase exponentially
with every step. You will be so exhausted that you'll need to
stop and take ten breaths between each step. Depending on the
weather, stay on the summit for between five minutes to an hour.
The descent should take about four hours, so you can be back
at camp before it gets dark. Many accidents and deaths occur
on the descent because people have used all their energy
getting to the top.

# 98. Work Abroad Illegally:

The European Commission estimates there are more than 8 million people working illegally in Europe alone, and about 15 percent of the EU's gross domestic product is generated by illegal workers. There are millions more working in the US and Asia. Governments worldwide are cracking down on employers, but there are still plenty of career opportunities in the black economy. From childcare to agricultural to construction work, moonlighting is a great way to fund your hobo lifestyle (see page 222).

## Free Flight Home

It's not just a blue collar thing either—with the global economic slowdown, middle class people such as lawyers and doctors have been moonlighting for cash, and not declaring income on the side.

It's all cash in hand, so you don't have to pay any tax or national insurance; the disadvantage is that unscrupulous employers can make you work long hours in unsafe conditions and pay you much lower wages for no job security. You may be toiling away in slave like conditions, but at least you don't have to give any of your earnings to the state, and if you get caught—pending the approval of new legislation—the company will have to pay the costs of repatriation—your flight home is free.

Governments talk tough about the hidden economy, but in practice the resources allocated at a local level to track down illegal workers is inadequate, so you'll probably be able to live and work abroad for many years, marry a local, and prosper. Working in the black economy is less risky than other crimes. For example, about one in 500 illegal workers are caught compared to thirty times this number of fraudulent benefit claimants. However, you must stay out of trouble: avoid situations that will bring you into contact with authorities— don't get caught speeding; if you are mugged, don't report it; if you fall ill, don't go to hospital; etc.

Here are three prime black economy jobs, where competition is fierce:

**CROP PICKING DOWN UNDER: the quality and availability of illegal fruit picking across Australia, varies greatly, but as a general rule, head for Victoria, New South Wales, South Australia or the south part of Western Australia between December and April, and then travel north to find construction work.**

**ROADSIDE HAWKER: selling people junk they don't want while they are trapped in their cars has always been a noble profession and a cornerstone of the black economy.**

COCKLE PICKING IN LANCASHIRE: Morecambe Bay in Lancashire is notoriously dangerous, with volatile rising tides and quicksand; but it is also a public fishery, so anyone can come collect the millions of pounds worth of cockles waiting to be dug up from the beach at low tide.

# 99. Have a Green Card Wedding:

Every day is a nice day for a green card wedding. Each year over 450,000 foreigners marry US citizens and apply for permanent residency status, or a green card, in the United States. The wedding is the easy part, but the visa application process is time consuming, confusing, and can be expensive.

If you are a US citizen, you can't just bring the fiancé or spouse you picked up during your travels into the United States; you have to go through a protracted application process first. The first step for applying for a green card is to submit either a fiancé visa petition or an immigrant visa petition. Your partner can't enter the country until the petition and other applications have been granted. Once the petition is approved, it is forwarded to the Immigrant Visa Department and then you must appear in person for a medical examination and a green card interview.

If your partner is in the US, you must file a Form I-130 with the Department of Homeland Security, US Citizenship and Immigration Services (USCIS), and make an application for adjustment of status (AOS) to permanent resident (form I-485).

# The Interview

The interview is supposed to be a chance for the INS officer to get to know your partner—but really it's to check that they're not a lunatic, terrorist, or con artist. If they screw this up, you'll both be turned in for a fraud interview, which will pick your relationship apart to make sure that you are living as a real couple and know the intimate details that only a co-habiting couple could know, such as:

**1. When she cuts her toe nails in the bath, does she leave then in a pile on the side of the bath, or put them in the trash?**

**2. Which grocery item does he always insist on adding to the weekly list that you always have to throw away when it expires?**

**3. What face does she make during orgasm?**

**4. He's in the desert, he sees a tortoise lying on its back, struggling, and he's not helping—why is that?**

**5. The two of you have a little boy; he shows her his butterfly collection, plus the killing jar. What is her reaction?**

**6. He's driving down Route 66; he turns and sees a chocolate chess set melting on the passenger seat. What does he do?**

**7. Tell me about her mother . . .**

# 100. Find a Hidden Tribe in the Amazon:

There are thought to be about 100 hidden tribes in the world, of which more than half are in the Brazilian and Peruvian Amazon. The best place to search for lost tribes is Brazil, where there are thought to be about forty, with another fifteen in Peru and a smattering in Bolivia, Paraguay, Ecuador, and Colombia. In other parts of the world, the lost tribes are in western Papua, parts of Indonesia, and North Sentinel Island in the Indian Ocean.

Very little is known about their society and technology, or the extent of their territory. However, they are presently under threat from logging and oil exploration, and the history of contact between indigenous tribes and the outside world has been unfavorable, if you do track down a tribe, don't expect a warm welcome. Isolated tribes are understandably willing to kill intruders to protect their lands.

**1. To reach a hidden tribe you will probably have to spend two weeks traveling on the river, followed by three weeks of continual bushwhacking through dense tropical jungle—the most hostile environment in the world after the Poles.**

2. Don't grab vines with your bare hands because many of them have thorns and can lacerate your palms; despite what you have seen in Tarzan movies, you can't always break open a vine and drink the water inside the stem. If the water is red, yellow, or milky, have a Diet Pepsi instead.

3. Remember, many species of poisonous snakes are remarkably small, and your biggest threats are from tiny insects, or infected cuts and bites.

4. Drink plenty of water, but go to the bathroom before you go to sleep, as the chance of getting bitten by malaria infected mosquitoes is exponentially proportional to the number of times you have to pee during the night.

5. If you see a freshly hacked sapling, dangling by a piece of bark lying across your path, this is a warning to stay away.

6. If you develop any form of sickness, even the common cold, turn back. These tribes have no resistance to even the everyday viruses that are an inconvenience for us, but a possible death sentence for them.

# 101. Avoid Obnoxious People While Traveling:

There are few itinerary tortures worse than sharing a ride with a talkative stranger. The phrase "nut-case on the bus" has become a term of quasi-endearment in our urban public transportation system. However, this inadequate and reductive cover-all cannot fully convey the horror of a sojourn spent staring into the jaws of obnoxious-stranger hell.

Here are four common reasons why complete strangers suddenly develop an overwhelming need to engage you in spoken language:

1. **They are lonely.**

2. **You have a sympathetic face.**

3. **They want to introduce you to Jesus.**

4. **Your hair is on fire.**

Here are five woefully inadequate strategies that may never-theless help to deter unwanted conversation:

## Create a Diversion

Crawl around the floor of the plane on all fours pretending to look for your wallet/contact lenses/prolapsed colon. This sends a powerful message that they should expect no money/attention/bowel control from you until further notice.

## Pretend to Be a Super Fan

Wear a pair of headphones; everyone will think you are lis-tening to music and won't disturb you. If you don't have head-phones, then hold a piece of fruit against your ear and shout "Yes! Go! Go!" People will think you are listening to a sports game on your novelty radio and leave you be.

## Become a Mormon

Invite Jesus into your life and use the name Donny Osmond in every other sentence (those on a mission to convert rarely waste time with ecumenical small talk).

## Pretend to Be French

Smile blankly, shrug and pout, then get out your cell phone and talk very loudly about how much you approve of agricultural subsidies and Saddam Hussein. The talkative stranger will think you are French and will leave you alone. He may even move seats.

## Safety Position

If nothing else works, assume the safety position: bring your knees up to your chest and hold them there with your arms. Bury your head in your hands and rock gently back and forth, moaning quietly.

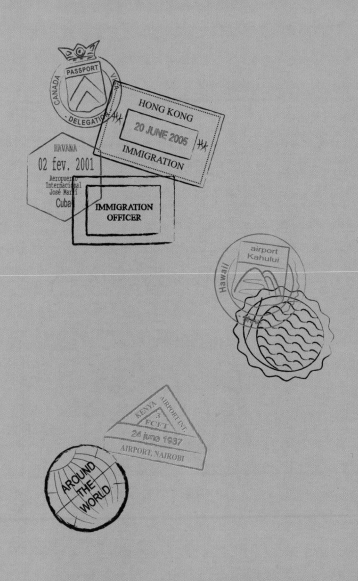